PARADISE LOST
Books IX and X

HARRAP'S ENGLISH CLASSICS

COMUS AND SOME SHORTER POEMS OF MILTON
Edited by E. M. W. TILLYARD, Litt.D., F.B.A., formerly Master of Jesus College, Cambridge, *and* PHYLLIS B. TILLYARD, M.A., Girton College, Cambridge

MILTON: PARADISE LOST: BOOKS I AND II
Edited by E. M. W. TILLYARD, Litt.D., F.B.A., formerly Master of Jesus College, Cambridge, *and* PHYLLIS B. TILLYARD, M.A., Girton College, Cambridge

MILTON: PARADISE LOST: BOOKS IX AND X
Edited by E. M. W. TILLYARD, Litt.D., F.B.A., formerly Master of Jesus College, Cambridge

CHAUCER: THE PROLOGUE TO THE CANTERBURY TALES
Edited by R. T. DAVIES, M.A., Lecturer in English Literature, Liverpool University

CHAUCER: THE KNIGHT'S TALE
Edited by J. A. W. BENNETT, M.A., D.Phil., Professor of Mediæval and Renaissance English in the University of Cambridge

CHAUCER: THE PARDONER'S TALE
Edited by NEVILL COGHILL, M.A., F.R.S.L., formerly Professor of English Literature in the University of Oxford, *and* CHRISTOPHER TOLKIEN, M.A., Fellow of New College, Oxford

CHAUCER: THE NUN'S PRIEST'S TALE
Edited by NEVILL COGHILL, M.A., F.R.S.L., formerly Professor of English Literature in the University of Oxford, *and* CHRISTOPHER TOLKIEN, M.A., Fellow of New College, Oxford

CHAUCER: THE MAN OF LAW'S TALE
Edited by NEVILL COGHILL, M.A., F.R.S.L., formerly Professor of English Literature in the University of Oxford, *and* CHRISTOPHER TOLKIEN, M.A., Fellow of New College, Oxford

TWENTIETH-CENTURY NARRATIVE POEMS
Compiled and edited by MAURICE WOLLMAN, M.A.

TEN TWENTIETH-CENTURY POETS
Edited by MAURICE WOLLMAN, M.A.

A BOOK OF MODERN PROSE
Edited by DOUGLAS BROWN, M.A., formerly of The Perse School, Cambridge

TWENTIETH-CENTURY SHORT STORIES
Edited by DOUGLAS R. BARNES, Senior English Master, Minchenden School, Southgate, *and* R. F. EGFORD, Senior English Master, Selhurst Grammar School

NINE TWENTIETH-CENTURY ESSAYISTS
Edited by HAROLD GARDINER, Senior English Master, Bedales School

TEN CONTEMPORARY POETS
Compiled and edited by MAURICE WOLLMAN, M.A.

STORIES IN MODERN VERSE
Compiled and edited by MAURICE WOLLMAN, M.A.

EIGHT MODERN AMERICAN POETS
Compiled and edited by C. W. GILLAM

Milton

PARADISE LOST
Books IX and X

EDITED WITH AN INTRODUCTION AND NOTES BY
E. M. W. TILLYARD Litt.D., F.B.A.

HARRAP   LONDON

First published in Great Britain 1960
by GEORGE G. HARRAP & CO. LTD
182-184 High Holborn, London WC1V 7AX

Reprinted: 1962 *(twice);* 1963; 1964; 1965; 1966;
1969; 1972; 1975

Printed in Great Britain by
Redwood Burn Limited
Trowbridge & Esher

PREFACE

In preparing the notes of this edition the following books have been found especially useful: Allan H. Gilbert's *A Geographical Dictionary of Milton* and the editions of A. W. Verity and Merritt Y. Hughes.

E.M.W.T.

*N*ow the serpent was more subtil than any beast of the field which the Lord God had made. And he said unto the woman, Yea, hath God said, Ye shall not eat of every tree of the garden?

And the woman said unto the serpent, We may eat of the fruit of the trees of the garden:

But of the fruit of the tree which is in the midst of the garden, God hath said, Ye shall not eat of it, neither shall ye touch it, lest ye die.

And the serpent said unto the woman, Ye shall not surely die:

For God doth know that in the day ye eat thereof, then your eyes shall be opened, and ye shall be as gods, knowing good and evil.

And when the woman saw that the tree was good for food, and that it was pleasant to the eyes, and a tree to be desired to make one wise, she took of the fruit thereof, and did eat, and gave also unto her husband with her; and he did eat.

And the eyes of them both were opened, and they knew that they were naked; and they sewed fig leaves together, and made themselves aprons.

And they heard the voice of the Lord God walking in the garden in the cool of the day: and Adam and his wife hid themselves from the presence of the Lord God amongst the trees of the garden.

And the Lord God called unto Adam, and said unto him, Where art thou?

And he said, I heard thy voice in the garden, and I was afraid, because I was naked; and I hid myself.

And he said, Who told thee that thou wast naked? Hast thou eaten of the tree, whereof I commanded thee that thou shouldest not eat?

And the man said, The woman whom thou gavest to be with me, she gave me of the tree, and I did eat.

And the Lord God said unto the woman, What is this that thou hast done? And the woman said, The serpent beguiled me, and I did eat. And the Lord God said unto the serpent, Because thou hast done this, thou art cursed above all cattle, and above every beast of the field; upon thy belly shalt thou go, and dust shalt thou eat all the days of thy life:

And I will put enmity between thee and the woman, and between thy seed and her seed; it shall bruise thy head, and thou shalt bruise his heel.

Unto the woman he said, I will greatly multiply thy sorrow and thy conception; in sorrow thou shalt bring forth children; and thy desire shall be to thy husband, and he shall rule over thee.

And unto Adam he said, Because thou hast hearkened unto the voice of thy wife, and hast eaten of the tree, of which I commanded thee, saying, Thou shalt not eat of it: cursed is the ground for thy sake; in sorrow shalt thou eat of it all the days of thy life;

Thorns also and thistles shall it bring forth to thee; and thou shalt eat the herb of the field;

In the sweat of thy face shalt thou eat bread, till thou return unto the ground; for out of it wast thou taken: for dust thou art, and unto dust shalt thou return.

And Adam called his wife's name Eve; because she was the mother of all living.

Unto Adam also and to his wife did the Lord God make coats of skins, and clothed them.

Genesis iii, 1–21

CONTENTS

INTRODUCTION

1. The Initial Difficulties

IT is futile to pretend that *Paradise Lost* as a whole is easy reading; and Books Nine and Ten are quite as exacting as any of the others. But a great deal of modern poetry is just as difficult; and even poetry that is superficially easy cannot, if it is more than minor verse, be appreciated fully without the cost of some effort. And far more important than the question whether a given poem is easy reading or not is the other question: whether it provides a rich return for any trouble expended. It is a question that applies just as surely to Eliot's *Four Quartets* or Pound's *Cantos* as to Milton's *Paradise Lost*. Though, in my experience, few readers today believe that Pound's *Cantos* justify the amount of effort required for the understanding of them, a great many believe that the *Four Quartets* do so; and, having that faith, are willing or even delighted to spend time and effort in their study. What makes Books Nine and Ten of *Paradise Lost* both difficult and repaying is their complexity. They are the central books of the poem and they illustrate Milton's total range. They are at once tragic, comic, tender, satirical, dulcet, grotesque, and noble, and they require an alert and adaptable mind for their appreciation. For this reason they are more exacting and less often prescribed for school use than Books One and Two, which with the terrible picture of Hell, the gigantic figure of Satan, and the realistic debate of the infernal peers make an immediate impression and require a less developed power of adaptation. But in the end Books Nine and Ten are quite as rewarding, if not more so; and it is not unfair to exact from schoolboys in the highest forms a quite considerable effort in studying them.

It is sometimes said that in understanding *Paradise Lost* the modern reader is at a disadvantage compared with the reader of fifty or a hundred years ago. This is but partly true; and if the modern reader is at a disadvantage in some ways he is better equipped in others. He knows the Bible and the Classics less well and will be less at home with Milton's allusions; he is less familiar with the traditional epic form and may be troubled with Milton's machinery. But he is less open to the mistake of separating the thought or the theology from the poetry; and he has learnt, through the complexities of modern verse, to respond more quickly than his predecessor to changes in aim and quality within a single poem. Thus, any idea that it was once fair to expect schoolboys to cope with *Paradise Lost* and that now it is unfair, is false. The difficulties are different but in amount very much the same.

Of the difficulties which I have said a modern reader finds in *Paradise Lost* perhaps the chief is the traditional epic form. In writing an introduction to some of Milton's short poems I said that the conventions of the modern detective story gave some sort of comparison with the pastoral convention which Milton used in

writing *Lycidas*. The best modern comparison I can
think of with the inherited form of the epic is the
British Coronation Service. That service is antique, in
some ways strange, but it possesses an awe and a mys-
tery that render any serious departure from its traditional form unthinkable. It would be easier to destroy
it than to change it. *Paradise Lost* is strictly in the
tradition of the classical epic; and Milton was strictly
in harmony with the temper of his age when he chose
to follow that tradition. Spenser, writing his *Faerie
Queene* in the age of Elizabeth in deliberate emulation
of Virgil's *Aeneid*, was free to depart widely from the
form of the classical epic; but during the seventeenth
century there arose in Europe the notion that in order
to do better than the ancients you had to follow their
lead; you had to abide by the rules of the various literary games they had played. This notion grew up in
Italy in the century before; and it was thought that
Tasso's *Jerusalem Delivered*, which used all the conventions of the classical epic, had got closer to the quality
of Homer and Virgil than any epic of modern times.
Milton wrote *Paradise Lost* in emulation of these three
poets and in so doing he committed himself to following, as it were, a certain ritual. Like parts of the
Coronation Service, parts of Milton's ritual in *Paradise Lost* may appear a little odd to a modern, but he
could not possibly have left them out; to do so would,
in the eyes of his contemporaries, have been a scandal.

The special difficulty of Books Nine and Ten of
Paradise Lost is their relation to the Bible. There are of
course constant references to the Bible throughout the
poem, but only in these books does Milton draw heavily

on the Bible for his story. The account of creation in Book Seven is indeed based on *Genesis* but it is vastly expanded and does not owe a great deal to the wording of its original. But the accounts of temptation, fall, and judgement are comparatively ample in *Genesis*; and Milton, living when he did, felt an obligation towards them that is difficult for us now to understand. The myth of the eating of the forbidden fruit still retains its attraction, for it speaks to something deep in our natures, but we feel differently about the actual way in which the myth was told in Scripture. Protestants of Milton's day, convinced of the inspiration of every word of the Bible, felt a special awe for the exact way of recounting this especially momentous part of it. Milton allowed for that awe, when he came to certain crucial parts of the story, by using, as far as his verse permitted, the very words of Scripture. Such passages may strike a modern reader as flat and out of keeping with the poetic context, and he has to understand that this is exactly what they would not have been to a contemporary reader. The bare words of Scripture would have an awe and a dignity beyond any mere poetising. The best way to meet this changed feeling for the text of Scripture is to be absolutely familiar with the relevant parts of *Genesis*, indeed to have them almost by heart. Such familiarity will give the passages a special character, will mark them off from other things not known in that way, and put the modern reader in the way of grasping the peculiar feelings of a seventeenth century one. In writing my notes I have assumed that those who use them are thoroughly versed in the relevant portion of *Genesis*.

2. Milton's Epic Plans

MILTON did not reach the idea of an epic on the fall of man at one stride; and we happen to know something of the processes through which he did reach it. There is evidence that, like Wordsworth and Keats, Milton consciously dedicated himself to poetry at a specific moment of his life. This was at the age of twenty-one; and we need not doubt that from that moment his ambitions included what was then universally considered the highest reach of poetry, the writing of an epic. Further, we know that the kind of epic Milton contemplated was both patriotic and religious. Virgil had celebrated Rome in the *Aeneid*; Milton would celebrate England as his predecessor, Spenser, had done. The great heroic events in English history were, for Milton and most of his English contemporaries, the emergence of England from civil war through the energies of the Tudors, the assertion of religious and national independence through the Reformation, and the defence and establishment of this assertion through the defeat of the Spanish Armada. Milton, again like Virgil, did not intend to use a contemporary setting through which to set forth recent events; but, as Virgil had gone back to the earliest myths about Rome, so Milton proposed to go back to the days of Arthur, with whom the Welsh house of Tudor claimed a mythical connection. In his Latin poem *Mansus*, written at Naples when he was about thirty, he speaks of his poetic plans and of making Arthur and the Round Table, with the defeat of the Saxons, his subject. We can be sure that Arthur would have stood both for a Christian king and for the Tudors, while the heathen Saxons would have stood both for the Turkish infidels that still threatened Europe and the Catholic enemies of English Protestantism. Further, explicit references to recent events would have been introduced through the medium of prophecy, in accordance with the practice of Virgil and Spenser.

The beginnings of the Civil War in 1639 both cut short Milton's European travels and held up his plans for an epic. He had no doubt which side he was on; and in the early days of the war he believed that a Parliamentary victory over the tyrannical Bishops, corrupters of the crown, would bring in a great spiritual betterment throughout the land. And he pictured himself as the poet who should celebrate the victory. It was in these early years of the Civil War, when Milton was living in London and conducting a small private school, that he seems to have had a notion of writing a poem on the fall of man. In the library of Trinity College, Cambridge there is preserved a manuscript containing the text of most of Milton's shorter poems, and jottings concerning future poetic work. These jottings consist of plans for a play or plays; and among many subjects that of Paradise Lost is the most prominent. There is no evidence that Milton meant to substitute a play on the fall of man for the epic on Arthur he had contemplated. On the contrary, he tells us in an autobiographical passage in *Reason of Church Government*, one of his pamphlets against the Bishops, that he is

thinking simultaneously of epic, tragedy, and the formal
ode as outlets for his high, patriotic, poetical plans.

After 1642, the year when Milton wrote *Reason of
Church Government*, and till 1655, when he began on
Paradise Lost, we have no evidence concerning his
plans for poetry. What we can conjecture with certainty is that they depended on the turn of national
events. As long as Milton had faith in his countrymen
and in the leaders of his side in the Civil War he could
contemplate a poem of heroic action, with a hero like
Arthur or Alfred the Great. But when he found that
the victorious Presbyterians were as illiberal and tyrannical as the Episcopalians and when he found his
countrymen feebly going back on their righteous hostility to the house of Stuart, he could no longer put his
heart into the kind of patriotic epic that had been the
rule in the Renaissance. Repudiating nationalism, he
went back to the old medieval theme that antedated the
rise of nationalism in Europe, the theme of Everyman,
of man in general fought for by the powers of good and
evil. That indeed is the innermost theme of *Paradise
Lost*. Though the narrative is based on the beginning
of the *Book of Genesis*, Adam and Eve are hero and
heroine, standing for Everyman and Everywoman, and
God defeats Satan in the battle for their souls.

What, then, we can be certain of is that between
1642 and 1655 Milton altered his conception of the sort
of subject that was apt to his epic and that the subject
he had once intended for a play was now found to
serve for a narrative. It was between these years too
that a great misfortune overtook him, his loss of sight.
But it was a misfortune that had its advantages. On

account of it the exacting post he held under Crom-
well's government became almost a nominal one; and
he at last had leisure to give most of his mind to
poetry, as he had been unable to do since his return
from Italy in 1639. At the age of forty-six he could
settle to the work he had had in mind since the age of
thirty-one.

How Milton composed *Paradise Lost*, in what years
he wrote the different books, we have no means of
judging. All we know is that he probably began
serious work on it in 1655 and that it was first printed
in 1667.

3. The Theme of "Paradise Lost"

I HAVE said that when Milton abandoned his idea of
a martial, patriotic epic he turned to the medieval subject of Everyman and displayed Adam and Eve fought
ever by the powers of good and evil. This is true as far
as it goes, but in depicting the fight Milton also gave
his version of the essential scheme of Christian theology and of the course of world history; he made his
subject as wide-embracing as it is possible to imagine.
Among his epic predecessors only Dante had included
so much. Further, Milton was vividly aware that the
present moment, life as actually lived now, was part of
the eternal process. Adam and Eve are not only figures
in the Old Testament and types of humanity at large;
they are types also of ourselves now. Nowhere is this
more evident than at the end of the poem, which describes Adam and Eve expelled by God's angels from

Paradise and left to make the best of life outside it.
These are the last five lines:

> Some natural tears they dropped, but wiped them soon;
> The world was all before them, where to choose
> Their place of rest, and Providence their guide:
> They hand in hand, with wand'ring steps and slow,
> Through Eden took their solitary way.

Adam and Eve are no longer archetypal, heroic figures.
They are ordinary man and woman, faced with the
ordinary problems of life in this world, granted wide
choice of good and evil on their own initiative, prone
to err and yet free to correct error by reliance on God.
But even in the opening books, where the scene is Hell,
where there is no human character and the setting is
deliberately alien to that of normal humanity on earth,
Milton succeeds in humanizing his theme. Though his
devils are figures with superhuman proportions, their
minds work like human minds, and their deliberations
are on the pattern of human politics. Further, in his
comparisons Milton constantly lets human history and
ordinary life into the context of Hell. His devils turn
out to be the heathen gods of the Old Testament and
of classical mythology, and as such they point to whole
areas of history. In the similes we have our attention
turned to homely things that were quite accepted and
commonplace in Milton's day: to benighted fishermen,
to the pipes of an organ, to a peasant with his supersti-
tious belief in fairies, to arguments on predestination
and free will. Just as the *Aeneid* was about the Rome of
Augustus as well as about the great workings of fate
that created Rome in the beginning and built up its
greatness, so is *Paradise Lost* about life as lived now in

Milton's time as well as about the great scheme under which all life was created and is transacted. And where Milton triumphs is in making the two themes inseparable: for him life today is also life in eternity.

4. The Scheme of "Paradise Lost"

THERE is little story involved in what I have called the theme of *Paradise Lost*. But Milton chose to express his theme not by direct exposition, as in a sermon, but through a verse narrative; and this choice meant a story.

Being virtually compelled through the public opinion of the age in which he lived to tell his story in the manner of the classical writers of epic, he must concentrate his action into a small span and include things outside that span through the methods of retrospective narrative and of prophecy. His theme was mankind in its complete historical setting fought over by the powers of good and evil. In this fight there were several stages. Taking the creation of the angels for granted and any ages of their undivided loyalty to God we care to imagine, we can say that, in the theological scheme Milton inherited and used, the first event in the fight was Satan's revolt in Heaven, which detached a portion of the angels to his side. After that revolt there was war in Heaven, at the end of which Satan and his crew were thrown out and fell through Chaos into Hell, which God had made out of part of Chaos to receive them. Meanwhile, God created the universe and its occupants, vegetable, animal, and human, as narrated at the beginning of the Bible. He gives the two first human beings, Adam and Eve, a garden to live in and with it the freedom of everything except the fruit of a single tree. In forbidding them to eat this fruit he tests their souls with a view to saving them. But he allows Satan to try to seduce them, and Satan succeeds. Thus Adam and Eve and their descendants are corrupted. Not completely, however, for the earth still contains a few virtuous men. But mankind cannot shed its corruption by its own efforts; hence, so far, Satan has had the best of the fight. God retaliates by submitting his son to the abasement of human incarnation. Having become man Christ can act as man's proxy and deal with Satan. He defeats Satan first by resisting his temptations in the wilderness and second by redeeming, through the gift of his own life on the cross, the loss of life Adam incurred through disobeying God's command in the garden. Mankind is now free to obtain salvation and everlasting life if it chooses to profit by Christ's sacrifice.

In this scheme of cosmic history there are four decisive acts: the revolt of Satan, the disobedience of man, Christ's resistance to Satan's temptations in the wilderness, and Christ's redeeming death. To any one wishing to recount the whole of world history as related to the scheme the first of these decisive acts would be inconvenient as coming too early in the series and as leaving so much of the total happenings in the future, not to be dealt with except through prophecy. Milton chose the second act for his principal poem and the third for his shorter narrative poem, *Paradise Regained*. Before his day there had been narrative poems on the crucifixion; the noblest rendering of it in English being certain parts of Langland's *Piers Plowman*. Langland put his greatest stress on the immediate consequence of the crucifixion as recorded in medieval legend, the so-called Harrowing (*i.e.*, subduing) of Hell. The legend was an expansion of the sentence in the Apostles' Creed, "he descended into Hell"; and it recounted Christ's breaking through the gates of Hell and releasing Adam and Eve from their prison, where they had been captive for 4000 years. Christ's act brought full circle the process that began with the original temptation in Paradise. By Milton's day the legend of the Harrowing of Hell, which had meant so much to the Middle Ages and which lent itself so well to dramatic treatment, had lost favour with Catholics and Protestants alike. It was not really available for him.

Milton, then, chose the disobedience and fall of man as the central acts round which to group, first, the drama of good and evil fighting for Everyman and, second, the course of world-history. But you cannot understand what he was doing unless you see that in these central acts he included the repentance and the virtual salvation of Adam and Eve, anticipating the redemptive process which, strictly speaking, did not take place till the Incarnation. By taking this liberty Milton was able vastly to extend the scope of his poem. Aristotle in his *Poetics* said that the best kind of tragic plot contains what he calls *peripeteia*, a word which a recent translator has rendered by *irony*. There is *peripeteia* when events which seem to tend in one direction actually take another. Milton must have followed the orthodox scholarly opinion of his day in thinking that most of

the things that were advisable in tragedy were advisable in the epic also. Now, by enlarging the scope
of the acts round which everything else is grouped
Milton was able to contrive a great irony, which domi-
nates his central episodes and has its effect on the rest
of the poem from the very beginning. The irony is
that the action that seems to lead to destruction, the
disobedience of Adam and Eve, and which does indeed
cause terrible havoc and suffering, unexpectedly has a
happy issue in their repentance and in their forgiveness
by God. And the irony is at the expense of Satan. He
had revolted from God and he concluded that if he
could persuade Adam and Eve to revolt, they, like
him, must be quite perverted to evil. He forgot that
his own crime was worse than theirs: it was entirely of
his own choosing; while theirs was partly the fault of
himself, who deceived them. Satan then is thwarted in
his fight through this *peripeteia*: what appeared to him
inevitably to lead one way actually led another. The
forces of good have won, and the souls of Adam and
Eve have been saved, as may be saved the souls of any
mortals who genuinely seek the salvation offered. In
this way *Paradise Lost* is not, as often thought, an
utterly tragic book with a pessimistic view of life. Good
does thwart evil. And yet the price Adam and his
descendants have had to pay for their crimes is great.
Sin and Death have indeed entered the word; and Paradise is no longer the crown of a happy existence but
the reward of humble endurance. Milton is acutely
aware of the inextricable interlocking of good and ill
in life as actually experienced.

5. The Construction of "Paradise Lost"

MILTON could have treated his theme in different ways;
and I go on to describe the way he disposed it.

Writing in the mode of the classical epic, Milton
begins his story in the middle of the total action. The
bad angels have already revolted and been defeated,
and God has already created Hell and the universe,
when Satan recovers consciousness and raises his head
from the fiery lake in which he is lying helpless. After
he has roused himself and his fellows and inspired them
with new courage, further action is made to hinge on
the rumour, current in Heaven before the angels fell,
that God was about to create a new kind of being. The
devils decide that the best way to carry on the war
against God is to seek to corrupt this new creation.
Satan is entrusted with the mission and meets his offspring, Sin and Death, at Hell's gate. They band themselves into a Trinity, which corresponds to and parodies
the Trinity of Heaven. Satan travels through Chaos to
the borders of light and sees the towers of Heaven and
the universe hanging from it by a chain. This ends the
first two books. But not only do these books promote
the plot; they also constitute a single motive, or in
musical phrase a movement. The motive is that of Hell
or of the complex of evil forces that is seeking to ruin
Everyman or Adam and Eve.

The third book opens with a long invocation of
light, symbol of the divine and the good, which marks

the statement of the second motive, Heaven. The felicity
of Heaven is described so as to match the miseries of
Hell; and, as Satan offered to go out alone to corrupt
mankind, so the Son offers to undergo a lonely incarnation in order to save it. Having described Heaven,
Milton continues the journey of Satan till he penetrates
the globe of the universe that contains the stars and
the planets and Earth in the centre, and lands on the
Earth.

It is now time for the human protagonists to be introduced; and in the fourth book Milton describes the
garden of Paradise and its human and animal inhabit-
tants, letting us know as he does this that Adam and
Eve are prohibited the use of a single tree in the garden.
Meanwhile Satan, disguised, enters the garden and
when Eve is asleep, insinuates an evil dream into her
ear. The guardian-angels set to watch discover him and
drive him out. So ends his first attempt to corrupt Eve.

Satan having been foiled, there is a pause in the
action, and Milton uses it for narrating past events.
The fifth and sixth books contain the visit of the Archangel Raphael to Paradise and the account he gives
Adam and Eve of the revolt and fall of the angels.
Though Raphael's visit extends for two more books,
Milton in his prologue to the seventh tell us that now
his stage is purely earthly; he has done with his vaster
setting; the rest of the poem centres on man. So now
Adam sets the pace and wants to know how the universe in which he dwells came into being. Raphael
recounts the six days of creation. In the eighth book
Adam asks more questions about the universe and then
recounts what happened to him since his first dawn of

consciousness. After which Raphael, having earnestly
warned Adam not to transgress God's prohibition,
returns to Heaven.

The main action is resumed in the ninth book and
reaches its crisis in it and in the tenth. With the crisis
comes a change of tone, to which Milton points in his
prologue to Book Nine. There he says that he is
changing his former style to tragic; and we do indeed
now feel ourselves right in the centre of real human
experience. Satan, disguised as a serpent, renews his
attack. He has the luck to find Eve alone and by lies
and flattery persuades her to eat the forbidden fruit.
Adam, finding her, eats also, and they are both in-
criminated. The fruit first intoxicates and then leaves
them disillusioned. The ninth book ends with a quarrel
and mutual recrimination. Satan to all appearances has
triumphed. But the main action has been but half transacted. The Son goes to Paradise to pass sentence on
Adam and Eve for their sin. He condemns them to
hardships on earth followed by death; but he also pities
and clothes them. Then the effects of man's fall show
themselves. The climate changes, the animals make war
on one another, Sin and Death build a causeway
through Chaos giving easy transit between Hell's
mouth and the entrance to the universe. Adam falls
into despair on seeing these happenings and thinks
himself lost for ever. Then Eve decides that to be at
variance with Adam is intolerable and wishes to take
all the blame on herself. Adam at first rebuffs her but
in the end, helped unwittingly by God's grace and not
in himself totally corrupted by his disobedience, admits
his own fault too, and they are reconciled. This act of

common humility is the salvation of Adam and Eve; and the tenth book ends with their asking God's pardon

with tears
Watering the ground, and with their sighs the air
Frequenting, sent from hearts contrite, in sign
Of sorrow unfeigned and humiliation meek.

Once Adam and Eve repent, the issue is certain, and the last two books deal almost entirely with future events. God, having accepted the pair's contrition, sends Michael, the great warrior archangel, to grant them a prophetic vision of the world's history. They see a series of tableaux of the main events described in *Genesis* up to the Flood; the point at which the eleventh book ends. Then in the twelfth and last book Michael summarizes history in his own words from the Flood till the day of doom, the happenings recounted in the New Testament included. Adam realizes now the nature of things and he accepts it; he has learnt obedience; he knows that Christian humility is stronger in the end than Satanic pride. And Adam and Eve are fortified with this knowledge when Michael leaves them, and his guard of angels expel them from Paradise to seek their fortune in the wider world.

6. Milton's Cosmos

THOUGH Milton was skilled in vague suggestive pictures, he was quite clear on the configuration of his universe. I do not mean that Milton believed these things literally. He lived in the pre-scientific age when the limits of belief were far less sharply defined than they came to be in the nineteenth century. People then did not always trouble to distinguish between actual happenings and acceptable metaphor. Certainly Milton did not believe literally in the geography of his Hell or in the physical embodiment of Sin. What I mean is that within the poem the imagined landscape is precise and needs to be realized for its proper appreciation.

One cannot describe Milton's cosmos simply because it was in process of growth during the course of the poem. We have to imagine a time when the sum of created things consisted of Heaven or the empyrean,

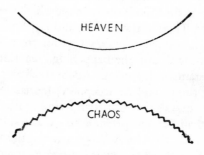

bounded by a crystal wall, and, at an indeterminate distance below it, the dark mass of Chaos, the confused and jarring material of possible future creation. Between the two was an open region enjoying heaven's light, and, as Satan found in his journey described at the end of the second book, there was a frontier, where chaos thinned out and neither darkness nor light but twilight prevailed. The first diagram illustrates this state of the cosmos.

When the bad angels were expelled from Heaven

God created a prison, Hell, to receive them. It was
situated at the very bottom of Chaos and it was vaulted
over and closed at the top of the vault with gates. The
diagram then has to be changed as follows:

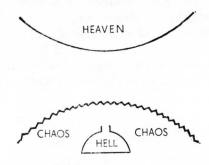

The final act of creation was for God to take more
of the material of Chaos and to create the universe.
There is no need to describe here the internal mechan-
ism of the universe with the earth in the middle and
the concentric spheres with the planets and fixed stars
around, for it does not concern the books of *Paradise
Lost* in question. But the reader needs to know that
the universe was enclosed by a solid shell, that there
was an opening at the top of this shell, through which
the angels and later the devils could pass in order to
visit mankind, and that a golden chain connected the
universe with Heaven. We thus get the third diagram
as shown on the next page. Last of all, as we are told
in Book Two it is destined to happen, Sin and Death
after the fall of man build a causeway from Hell-gate
through Chaos to the point on the outside of the universe where there is the opening that leads inside.

Though the devils fell in confusion, Milton makes
them keep their different stations when they have risen
from the fiery lake. This is most evident when he pictures the leaders approaching Satan, as he stands by
the lake-side, singly, in order of seniority. Milton does
this because he still retains traces of the medieval idea
of a world organized with a kind of mathematical regu-
larity. The feudal organization of society was both
elaborate and accurately graded. And if human society
was thus graded, so had heavenly society to be. In the

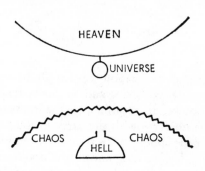

most generally accepted account the angels were
arranged in a fixed order according to their natural
capacity to receive the divine essence. Those of inferior
capacity received it through the medium of their supe-
riors. There were three main classes of angels and each
class had three divisions. The highest class was contemplative and consisted of Seraphs, Cherubs, and
Thrones. The next class was partly contemplative and
partly active and consisted of Dominations, Virtues,
and Powers. More active still was the third class, and

it consisted of Principalities, Archangels, and Angels.
It is this lowest division, the Angels, who go on God's
errands. Corresponding to the nine divisions of angels
were nine of devils. Milton made use of some of this
medieval lore, but by his day the old medieval preci-
sion had been abandoned. Although he was in the
medieval tradition in making Satan, Beelzebub, and
Mammon important individual devils, he abandoned
the medieval classes of devils and uses the angelic
classes for fallen as well as unfallen angels. Also in
using those classes he alters the order of their dignity.
He makes the Archangels the highest division, higher
than the Seraphs and Cherubs. Nor does he distinguish the relative importance of Thrones, or Virtues,
or Powers; and he can make the word "Powers" cover
all classes of angel. He was in fact more interested in
the idea of there being an order than in the precise
nature of it. Hence his frequent use of the words *hier-
arch* and *hierarchy*. When he uses those words he wants
us to think of the principle of orderly arrangement
throughout the cosmos.

Not only did medieval people like to think of all
creation arranged in a sequence, they liked also to find
correspondences everywhere. I have just mentioned
the nine orders of devils corresponding to the nine
orders of angels. They thought it fitting that as the
Devil corrupted man in the garden of Paradise and
caused him to exchange Paradise for a wilderness, so
Christ, the second Adam, defeated the Devil's temptations in the wilderness and restored Paradise to the
first Adam. Milton's invention of the trinity of Satan,
Sin, and Death to correspond to the Christian Trinity

illustrates the same habit of mind. It is a valuable habit, for it makes for tightness of poetic structure.

So much for the nature of *Paradise Lost* in general. I pass to some special points in Books Nine and Ten.

7. The Crisis

IN Section 4, on the scheme of *Paradise Lost*, I stated categorically that the poem was founded on a great irony; that Books Nine and Ten make a single unit; and that the real crisis was the reconciliation of Adam and Eve and not just the Fall by itself. I have argued this at length in the section of my *Studies in Milton* called the *Crisis of " Paradise Lost,"* and I think the argument important for seeing the poem in its proper proportions; but I must warn the reader that it has long been usual to confine the crisis to the eating of the fruit and to look on the events of Book Ten as a mere consequence of the one vital act. Given this immense weight, the story of the Fall as told by Milton has been thought not quite to support it, as being too casually narrated. Neither Eve nor Adam put up a very serious resistance to their respective temptations: they here lack the heroic touch; and through that lack they allow Satan, who is not the hero, to usurp most of the heroic spirit. Such weakness at the apparent crisis somewhat impairs the quality of the whole poem. But if, as I hold, the Fall is not the real climax but only the climax as imagined by Satan in his ignorance of God's ways, then it would be wrong if it were made overwhelmingly emphatic. By

keeping it toned down Milton was able to carry the
action on to the consequences of the Fall and to the
noble action of Adam and Eve in extricating themselves
from their dreadful predicament. That action, though
so simple and human and apparently small, was yet
more heroic than all the violent doings of Satan.

I believe that Milton himself hinted at the truth in
these matters within his poem. First, in the opening of
Book Nine he claimed that the "fortitude of patience
and heroic martyrdom" was better than the military
heroisms that were the subject of the old epics. Now
Adam ended by showing exactly that patience which
Milton mentioned. Second, there is the momentous
conversation between Adam and the Archangel
Michael at the end of the last book. (The last hundred
lines of the poem are among the greatest Milton wrote
and should be read by students of any parts of his
verse.) Here Adam tells Michael that he has now learnt
his lesson and that he will rest in God,

                                        with good
    Still overcoming evil, and by small
    Accomplishing great things, by things deemed weak
    Subverting wordly strong, and worldly wise
    By simply meek.

Again, Milton here puts in general terms what Adam
and Eve had shown by their deeds as narrated in the
last lines of Book Ten, and I have no doubt that he
meant us to make this cross-reference. If he did, there
can be no doubt where he intended the crisis to be
placed.

Milton told us the same thing, obliquely, through
the way he constructed Book Ten. In the notes I have

pointed to certain grotesque and monstrous qualities in some of the happenings after the Fall, for instance, in the accounts of the causeway built by Sin and Death from Hell to the universe and of the devils' eating the Dead Sea fruit. And he exploited these qualities in order to make more prominent the utterly different qualities of the scenes where Adam and Eve make up their quarrel by confessing their own faults instead of each blaming the other, and deciding to ask God's pardon. The very simple human emotions that govern these scenes are given immense emphasis by the grotesqueness and the monstrosity of the scenes they follow; Milton indicates that he meant us to give them the utmost weight.

8. The Fall

A GREAT deal has been written about the way Milton deals with the story of the Fall; and it would take too long to summarize all the theories on what exactly he meant. Instead, I shall confine myself to two matters: first, a difficulty that Milton incurred by choosing just this subject, and second the general significance that the story as treated by Milton can have for us today.

The story of the Fall as recounted in *Genesis* involves the passing from a state of innocence to a state of sin, and Milton seems to accept the need to deal with this transition. Naturally enough most critics have accepted Milton's acceptance. In doing so they have forgotten that the human mind cannot conceive a state of innocence that is at the same time human. It can observe the innocence of animals, an innocence lacking moral responsibility. But the supposed innocence of Adam and Eve has moral responsibility as its very core and is already aware of evil as well as good. No wonder if Milton has been blamed for failing to make the necessary transition convincing. Technically, Eve should be transformed the moment she takes a bite of the apple; but in reading Milton's account we feel that she was much the same person before and after the event. In actual fact, if we blame Milton we should do so for pretending to do an impossible job, not for failing to do it. The truth is that Adam and Eve in Milton's poem are not innocent but inexperienced and that the plot concerns not the loss of innocence but the acquisition of experience. Adam and Eve, disputing about whether Eve shall garden alone, are as fully human and "fallen" as they are when they accuse each other after the Fall, even though they are much more inexperienced. The plain fact is this. Milton was attracted to the story of the Fall because of its fame and its essential fascination; because of the immense authority of Scripture he could not openly revolt from the scriptural presentation of the story although it involved an impossibility; and he was forced to depart from Scripture while pretending to follow it. If you frankly accept Adam and Eve as ordinary if inexperienced human beings, you will find that Milton's treatment of their story presents no difficulties.

The myth of the Fall fascinates a modern chiefly because it can symbolize some stage in the evolution of

man. In the course of his history man may have attained
to states of comparative equilibrium. To upset such a
desirable state would be a kind of sin; and yet, if man
was to evolve, such an upsetting was necessary; man
had to violate his present state by a forbidden act.
Milton, lacking our knowledge of history, could not
consciously think of the story in that way; and anyhow
such a way of thinking would have been blasphemous.
He thought of the Fall differently, and yet in ways that
apply perfectly to present conditions of life.

Milton put the Fall in terms of disobedience to a
command the reason for which was not explained. And
this lack of explanation has been one reason why many
readers have condemned Milton's presentation of God.
By pronouncing an arbitrary taboo God, they think,
showed himself a tyrant. That was not at all Milton's
idea, for he accepted the arbitrary, unexplained command as necessary for testing the true validity of faith.
If all is explained, nothing remains that has to be
taken on pure trust; and something of that kind ought
to remain. All this corresponds most closely to the
human condition. We are confronted by many things
we cannot explain and which seem all wrong; but we
do no good by revolting against them, by arguing that
if these things are all wrong everything else must be.
The wise man does not revolt against the inexplicable
even if he dislikes it.

The nature of the disobedience of Adam and Eve,
Milton makes plain enough. It was pride, taking the
form of refusing to accept the limits of humanity as
ordained by God. Just as Satan aspired beyond the
angelic state to sheer godhead, so Eve aspired, through

the agency of the forbidden fruit, to reach a state beyond that enjoyable on earth. When Adam and Eve have eaten the fruit they vainly imagine themselves blossoming into a superhuman state. But at the end of the poem Adam, now regenerate, speaks of

> my fill
> Of knowledge, what this vessel can contain;
> Beyond which was my folly to aspire.

Disobedience then means not merely the breaking of a rule but disregarding the conditions of life, going against the very nature of things, refusing to come to terms with the laws of our environment. If this is disobedience, obedience is facing and accepting the facts; and man's true freedom is, having done so, to shape his life with all possible energy within the frame of that acceptance. Milton expressed this doctrine in more theological terms than most people would do today; but the doctrine is there and is as apt now as it was in the seventeenth century.

9. Prosody and Style

It is strange that school editions of *Paradise Lost* usually contain a section on the prosody, whereas school editions of Shakespeare's plays usually do not: as if Shakespeare wrote blank verse by nature and Milton on a preconceived metrical scheme. Nothing could be more mistaken. They both inherited a common metre and used it in the ways that best suited their purposes.

It is useful to know some system of prosody in order
to be able to describe different kinds of blank verse or
other kinds of metre; but that usefulness applies equally
to all verse. And more important than a knowledge of
a prosodical system is the ability to *read* a given piece
of blank verse: to get the emphasis and the pauses and
the weight of syllables right. These are things which, if
treated in an edition, would swell an introduction to
an inordinate length; and they should be the concern
of the teacher in co-operation with any pupils who
have a gift for such matters.

As for Milton's style, beware of making it out simpler than it is. Writers have called it sublime or latin-
ized or elaborate or what not, and up to a point they
have been right. But Milton never confined himself to
any set way of writing. Take his account of Moloch
in Book Two:

> His trust was with the Eternal to be deemed
> Equal in strength, and rather than be less
> Cared not to be at all; with that care lost
> Went all his fear: of God, or Hell, or worse
> He recked not.

Here Milton is emphatic enough; but how unadorned
and unlatinized and uninflated! None of the usual adjectives descriptive of his style fit the passage. And this
one example can serve to demonstrate the truth that
Milton is far too great and varied a poet to be bound
by easy generalizations. The right course is to take him
without rigid predispositions, to be open to what he
offers you, to enjoy him for what he is and not for
what you have been told, or have imagined before-
hand, he ought to be.

10. The Text

Paradise Lost was first published in 1667, in ten books; and there were new impressions of this first edition in the next two years. In 1674 Milton published a revised edition, introducing a few changes into the text and dividing the original Books Seven and Ten each into two so as to make twelve books in all after the manner of Virgil. The text here given is nearly always that of 1674, with spelling modernized and some changes in the punctuation.

11. Bibliography

The following books may be found useful for further reading:

Bush, Douglas, *Paradise Lost in our Time* (Oxford University Press, 1945).

Grierson, H. J. C., *Milton and Wordsworth* (Cambridge University Press, 1937).

Lewis, C. S., *A Preface to Paradise Lost* (Oxford University Press, 1942).

Muir, Kenneth, *John Milton* (Longmans, Green, 1955).

Raleigh, Walter, *Milton* (Edward Arnold, 1900).

Tillyard, E. M. W., *Milton* (Chatto and Windus, 1930). *Studies in Milton* (Chatto and Windus, 1951).

Warner, Rex, *John Milton* (Max Parrish, 1950).

Waldock, A. J. A., *Paradise Lost and its Critics* (Cambridge University Press, 1947).

PARADISE LOST

Book IX

No more of talk where god or angel guest
With man, as with his friend, familiar used
To sit indulgent and with him partake
Rural repast, permitting him the while
Venial discourse unblamed. I now must change   5
Those notes to tragic: foul distrust and breach
Disloyal on the part of man, revolt
And disobedience; on the part of Heaven,
Now alienated, distance and distaste,
Anger and just rebuke, and judgment given,   10
That brought into this World a world of woe,
Sin and her shadow Death, and Misery,
Death's harbinger. Sad task! yet argument
Not less but more heroic than the wrath
Of stern Achilles on his foe pursued   15
Thrice fugitive about Troy wall or rage
Of Turnus for Lavinia disespoused
Or Neptune's ire or Juno's, that so long
Perplexed the Greek and Cytherea's son;
If answerable style I can obtain   20
Of my celestial patroness, who deigns
Her nightly visitation unimplored
And dictates to me slumbering or inspires

Easy my unpremeditated verse;
Since first this subject for heroic song   25
Pleased me, long choosing and beginning late,
Not sedulous by nature to indite
Wars, hitherto the only argument
Heroic deemed, chief maistry to dissect
With long and tedious havoc fabled knights   30
In battles feigned (the better fortitude
Of patience and heroic martyrdom
Unsung), or to describe races and games
Or tilting furniture, emblazoned shields,
Impreses quaint, caparisons and steeds,   35
Bases and tinsel trappings, gorgeous knights
At joust and tournament; then marshalled feast
Served up in hall with sewers and seneshals:
The skill of artifice or office mean,
Not that which justly gives heroic name   40
To person or to poem. Me, of these
Nor skilled nor studious, higher argument
Remains, sufficient of itself to raise
That name, unless an age too late or cold
Climate or years damp my intended wing   45
Depressed; and much they may, if all be mine,
Not hers who brings it nightly to my ear.
    The sun was sunk, and after him the star
Of Hesperus, whose office is to bring
Twilight upon the Earth, short arbiter   50
'Twixt day and night, and now from end to end
Night's hemisphere had veiled the horizon round;
When Satan, who late fled before the threats
Of Gabriel out of Eden, now improved
In meditated fraud and malice, bent   55

On man's destruction, maugre what might hap
Of heavier on himself, fearless returned.
By night he fled and at midnight returned
From compassing the Earth; cautious of day,
Since Uriel, regent of the sun, descried 60
His entrance and forewarned the Cherubim
That kept their watch. Thence full of anguish driven,
The space of seven continued nights he rode
With darkness; thrice the equinoctial line
He circled, four times crossed the car of night 65
From pole to pole, traversing each colure;
On the eighth returned and on the coast averse
From entrance or cherubic watch by stealth
Found unsuspected way. There was a place
(Now not, though sin, not time, first wrought the
      change) 70
Where Tigris, at the foot of Paradise,
Into a gulf shot under ground, till part
Rose up a fountain by the Tree of Life.
In with the river sunk and with it rose
Satan, involved in rising mist; then sought 75
Where to lie hid. Sea he had searched and land
From Eden over Pontus and the pool
Mæotis, up beyond the river Ob;
Downward as far antarctic; and in length
West from Orontes to the ocean barred 80
At Darien, thence to the land where flows
Ganges and Indus. Thus the orb he roamed
With narrow search, and with inspection deep
Considered every creature, which of all
Most opportune might serve his wiles, and found 85
The serpent subtlest beast of all the field.

Him, after long debate, irresolute
Of thoughts revolved, his final sentence chose
Fit vessel, fittest imp of fraud, in whom
To enter, and his dark suggestions hide   90
From sharpest sight; for in the wily snake
Whatever sleights none would suspicious mark,
As from his wit and native subtlety
Proceeding, which, in other beasts observed,
Doubt might beget of diabolic power.   95
Active within beyond the sense of brute.
Thus he resolved but first from inward grief
His bursting passion into plaints thus poured:
    "O Earth, how like to Heaven, if not preferred
More justly, seat worthier of gods, as built   100
With second thoughts, reforming what was old!
For what god, after better, worse would build?
Terrestrial Heaven, danced round by other heavens,
That shine yet bear their bright officious lamps,
Light above light, for thee alone, as seems,   105
In thee concentring all their precious beams
Of sacred influence. As God in Heaven
Is centre yet extends to all, so thou
Centring receiv'st from all those orbs; in thee,
Not in themselves, all their known virtue appears   110
Productive in herb, plant, and nobler birth
Of creatures animate with gradual life
Of growth, sense, reason, all summed up in man.
With what delight could I have walked thee round,
If I could joy in aught, sweet interchange   115
Of hill and valley, rivers, woods, and plains,
Now land, now sea, and shores with forest crowned,
Rocks, dens, and caves! but I in none of these

Find place or refuge; and the more I see
Pleasure about me, so much more I feel   120
Torment within me, as from the hateful siege
Of contraries: all good to me becomes
Bane, and in Heaven much worse would be my state.
But neither here seek I, no, nor in Heaven
To dwell, unless by mastering Heaven's Supreme; 125
Nor hope to be myself less miserable
By what I seek, but others to make such
As I, though thereby worse to me redound:
For only in destroying I find ease
To my relentless thoughts; and, him destroyed   130
Or won to what may work his utter loss,
For whom all this was made, all this will soon
Follow, as to him linked in weal or woe:
In woe then, that destruction wide may range.
To me shall be the glory sole among   135
The infernal powers, in one day to have marred
What he, Almighty styled, six nights and days
Continued making, and who knows how long
Before had been contriving? though perhaps
Not longer than since I in one night freed   140
From servitude inglorious well nigh half
The angelic name, and thinner left the throng
Of his adorers. He, to be avenged
And to repair his numbers thus impaired—
Whether such virtue spent of old now failed   145
More angels to create, if they at least
Are his created, or to spite us more—
Determined to advance into our room
A creature formed of earth and him endow,
Exalted from so base original,   150

With heavenly spoils, our spoils. What he decreed
He effected: man he made and for him built
Magnificent this world, and Earth his seat;
Him lord pronounced, and, O indignity!
Subjected to his service angel wings 155
And flaming ministers to watch and tend
Their earthy charge. Of these the vigilance
I dread, and, to elude, thus wrapt in mist
Of midnight vapour glide obscure and pry
In every bush and brake, where hap may find 160
The serpent sleeping, in whose mazy folds
To hide me and the dark intent I bring.
O foul descent! that I, who erst contended
With gods to sit the highest, am now constrained
Into a beast, and, mixed with bestial slime, 165
This essence to incarnate and imbrute,
That to the highth of deity aspired.
But what will not ambition and revenge
Descend to? Who aspires must down as low
As high he soared, obnoxious first or last 170
To basest things. Revenge, at first though sweet,
Bitter ere long back on itself recoils.
Let it; I reck not, so it light well aimed
(Since higher I fall short) on him who next
Provokes my envy, this new favourite 175
Of Heaven, this man of clay, son of despite,
Whom, us the more to spite, his maker raised
From dust: spite then with spite is best repaid."
　　So saying, through each thicket, dank or dry,
Like a black mist low-creeping, he held on 180
His midnight search, where soonest he might find
The serpent. Him fast sleeping soon he found,

In labyrinth of many a round self-rolled,
His head the midst, well stored with subtle wiles:
Not yet in horrid shade or dismal den,   185
Nor nocent yet, but on the grassy herb,
Fearless, unfeared, he slept. In at his mouth
The Devil entered, and his brutal sense
In heart or head possessing, soon inspired
With act intelligential; but his sleep   190
Disturbed not, waiting close the approach of morn.
   Now, whenas sacred light began to dawn
In Eden on the humid flowers, that breathed
Their morning incense, when all things that breathe
From the Earth's great altar send up silent praise   195
To the creator and his nostrils fill
With grateful smell, forth came the human pair,
And joined their vocal worship to the quire
Of creatures wanting voice; that done, partake
The season, prime for sweetest scents and airs;   200
Then commune how that day they best may ply
Their growing work, for much their work outgrew
The hands' dispatch of two, gardening so wide:
And Eve first to her husband thus began:
   "Adam, well may we labour still to dress   205
This garden, still to tend plant, herb, and flower,
Our pleasant task enjoined; but, till more hands
Aid us, the work under our labour grows,
Luxurious by restraint: what we by day
Lop overgrown or prune or prop or bind   210
One night or two with wanton growth derides,
Tending to wild. Thou therefore now advise
Or hear what to my mind first thoughts present:
Let us divide our labours—thou where choice

Leads thee, or where most needs, whether to wind   215
The woodbine round this arbour or direct
The clasping ivy where to climb; while I,
In yonder spring of roses intermixed
With myrtle, find what to redress till noon.
For, while so near each other thus all day   220
Our task we choose, what wonder if so near
Looks intervene and smiles, or object new
Casual discourse draw on, which intermits
Our day's work, brought to little, though begun
Early, and the hour of supper comes unearned."   225
    To whom mild answer Adam thus returned:
"Sole Eve, associate sole, to me beyond
Compare above all living creatures dear,
Well hast thou motioned, well thy thoughts employed
How we might best fulfil the work which here   230
God hath assigned us, nor of me shalt pass
Unpraised; for nothing lovelier can be found
In woman than to study household good
And good works in her husband to promote.
Yet not so strictly hath our Lord imposed   235
Labour, as to debar us when we need
Refreshment, whether food or talk between
(Food of the mind) or this sweet intercourse
Of looks and smiles; for smiles from reason flow,
To brute denied, and are of love the food,   240
Love, not the lowest end of human life.
For not to irksome toil but to delight
He made us, and delight to reason joined.
These paths and bowers doubt not but our joint hands
Will keep from wilderness with ease, as wide   245
As we need walk, till younger hands ere long

Assist us. But if much converse perhaps
Thee satiate, to short absence I could yield;
For solitude sometimes is best society,
And short retirement urges sweet return.   250
But other doubt possesses me, lest harm
Befall thee severed from me; for thou know'st
What hath been warned us, what malicious foe,
Envying our happiness and of his own
Despairing, seeks to work us woe and shame   255
By sly assault; and somewhere nigh at hand
Watches, no doubt, with greedy hope to find
His wish and best advantage, us asunder,
Hopeless to circumvent us joined, where each
To other speedy aid might lend at need.   260
Whether his first design be to withdraw
Our feälty from God, or to disturb
Conjugal love, than which perhaps no bliss
Enjoyed by us excites his envy more;
Or this or worse, leave not the faithful side   265
That gave thee being, still shades thee and protects.
The wife, where danger or dishonour lurks,
Safest and seemliest by her husband stays,
Who guards her or with her the worst endures."
          To whom the virgin majesty of Eve,   270
As one who loves and some unkindness meets,
With sweet austere composure thus replied:
          "Offspring of Heaven and Earth, and all Earth's
               lord,
That such an enemy we have, who seeks
Our ruin, both by thee informed I learn   275
And from the parting Angel overheard,
As in a shady nook I stood behind,

Just then returned at shut of evening flowers.
But that thou shouldst my firmness therefore doubt
To God or thee, because we have a foe   280
May tempt it, I expected not to hear.
His violence thou fear'st not, being such
As we, not capable of death or pain,
Can either not receive or can repel.
His fraud is then thy fear; which plain infers   285
Thy equal fear that my firm faith and love
Can by his fraud be shaken or seduced:
Thoughts, which how found they harbour in thy
          breast,
Adam, misthought of her to thee so dear?"
     To whom with healing words Adam replied: 290
"Daughter of God and man, immortal Eve,
(For such thou art, from sin and blame entire)
Not diffident of thee do I dissuade
Thy absence from my sight but to avoid
The attempt itself, intended by our foe.   295
For he who tempts, though in vain, at least asperses
The tempted with dishonour foul, supposed
Not incorruptible of faith, not proof
Against temptation. Thou thyself with scorn
And anger wouldst resent the offered wrong,   300
Though ineffectual found; misdeem not then,
If such affront I labour to avert
From thee alone, which on us both at once
The enemy, though bold, will hardly dare,
Or, daring, first on me the assault shall light.   305
Nor thou his malice and false guile contemn
(Subtle he needs must be, who could seduce
Angels) nor think superfluous others' aid.

I from the influence of thy looks receive
Access in every virtue: in thy sight   310
More wise, more watchful, stronger, if need were
Of outward strength; while shame, thou looking on,
Shame to be overcome or overreached,
Would utmost vigour raise, and raised unite.
Why shouldst not thou like sense within thee feel 315
When I am present and thy trial choose
With me, best witness of thy virtue tried?"
    So spake domestic Adam in his care
And matrimonial love; but Eve, who thought
Less attributed to her faith sincere,   320
Thus her reply with accent sweet renewed:
    "If this be our condition thus to dwell
In narrow circuit straitened by a foe,
Subtle or violent, we not endued
Single with like defence wherever met,   325
How are we happy, still in fear of harm?
But harm precedes not sin. Only our foe,
Tempting, affronts us with his foul esteem
Of our integrity: his foul esteem
Sticks no dishonour on our front but turns   330
Foul on himself; then wherefore shunned or feared
By us? who rather double honour gain
From his surmise proved false, find peace within,
Favour from Heaven, our witness, from the event.
And what is faith, love, virtue, unassayed   335
Alone, without exterior help sustained?
Let us not then suspect our happy state
Left so imperfect by the maker wise
As not secure to single or combined.
Frail is our happiness, if this be so,   340

And Eden were no Eden, thus exposed."
   To whom thus Adam fervently replied:
"O woman, best are all things as the will
Of God ordained them; his creating hand
Nothing imperfect or deficient left   345
Of all that he created, much less man
Or aught that might his happy state secure,
Secure from outward force: within himself
The danger lies, yet lies within his power;
Against his will he can receive no harm.   350
But God left free the will; for what obeys
Reason is free, and reason he made right,
But bid her well be ware and still erect,
Lest, by some fair appearing good surprised,
She dictate false and misinform the will   355
To do what God expressly hath forbid.
Not then mistrust, but tender love, enjoins
That I should mind thee oft and mind thou me.
Firm we subsist yet possible to swerve,
Since reason not impossibly may meet   360
Some specious object by the foe suborned
And fall into deception unaware,
Not keeping strictest watch, as she was warned.
Seek not temptation then, which to avoid
Were better, and most likely if from me   365
Thou sever not: trial will come unsought.
Wouldst thou approve thy constancy, approve
First thy obedience; the other who can know,
Not seeing thee attempted, who attest?
But if thou think trial unsought may find   370
Us both securer than thus warned thou seem'st,
Go, for thy stay, not free, absents thee more;

Go in thy native innocence, rely
On what thou hast of virtue, summon all:
For God towards thee hath done his part; do
    thine."   375
  So spake the patriarch of mankind; but Eve
Persisted; yet submiss, though last, replied:
  "With thy permission then, and thus forewarned
Chiefly by what thine own last reasoning words
Touched only, that our trial, when least sought, 380
May find us both perhaps far less prepared,
The willinger I go, nor much expect
A foe so proud will first the weaker seek;
So bent, the more shall shame him his repulse."
   Thus saying, from her husband's hand her hand 385
Soft she withdrew and like a wood-nymph light,
Oread or Dryad, or of Delia's train,
Betook her to the groves; but Delia's self
In gait surpassed and goddess-like deport,
Though not as she with bow and quiver armed, 390
But with such gardening tools as art, yet rude,
Guiltless of fire, had formed, or angels brought.
To Pales or Pomona, thus adorned,
Likest she seemed: Pomona when she fled
Vertumnus, or to Ceres in her prime,   395
Yet virgin of Proserpina from Jove.
Her long with ardent look his eye pursued
Delighted, but desiring more her stay.
Oft he to her his charge of quick return
Repeated; she to him as oft engaged   400
To be returned by noon amid the bower,
And all things in best order to invite
Noontide repast or afternoon's repose.

O much deceived, much failing, hapless Eve,
Of thy presumed return! event perverse!   405
Thou never from that hour in Paradise
Found'st either sweet repast or sound repose;
Such ambush, hid among sweet flowers and shades,
Waited with hellish rancour imminent
To intercept thy way or send thee back   410
Despoiled of innocence, of faith, of bliss.
For now, and since first break of dawn, the fiend,
Mere serpent in appearance, forth was come
And on his quest, where likeliest he might find
The only two of mankind, but in them   415
The whole included race, his purposed prey.
In bower and field he sought, where any tuft
Of grove or garden-plot more pleasant lay,
Their tendance or plantation for delight,
By fountain or by shady rivulet   420
He sought them both but wished his hap might find
Eve separate. He wished, but not with hope
Of what so seldom chanced; when to his wish,
Beyond his hope, Eve separate he spies,
Veiled in a cloud of fragrance, where she stood,   425
Half-spied, so thick the roses bushing round
About her glowed, oft stooping to support
Each flower of tender stalk, whose head, though gay
Carnation, purple, azure, or specked with gold,
Hung drooping unsustained; them she upstays   430
Gently with myrtle band, mindless the while
Herself, though fairest unsupported flower,
From her best prop so far, and storm so nigh.
Nearer he drew and many a walk traversed
Of stateliest covert, cedar, pine, or palm;   435

Then voluble and bold, now hid, now seen,
Among thick-woven arborets and flowers
Imbordered on each bank, the hand of Eve:
Spot more delicious than those gardens feigned
Or of revived Adonis or renowned   440
Alcinous, host of old Laertes' son,
Or that, not mystic, where the sapient king
Held dalliance with his fair Egyptian spouse.
Much he the place admired, the person more.
As one who, long in populous city pent,   445
Where houses thick and sewers annoy the air,
Forth issuing on a summer's morn to breathe
Among the pleasant villages and farms
Adjoined, from each thing met conceives delight,
The smell of grain or tedded grass or kine   450
Or dairy, each rural sight, each rural sound;
If chance with nymph-like step fair virgin pass,
What pleasing seemed for her now pleases more,
She most and in her look sums all delight:
Such pleasure took the Serpent to behold   455
This flowery plat, the sweet recess of Eve
Thus early, thus alone. Her heavenly form
Angelic, but more soft and feminine,
Her graceful innocence, her every air
Of gesture or least action, overawed   460
His malice and with rapine sweet bereaved
His fierceness of the fierce intent it brought.
That space the evil one abstracted stood
From his own evil and for the time remained
Stupidly good, of enmity disarmed,   465
Of guile, of hate, of envy, of revenge.
But the hot hell that always in him burns,

Though in mid Heaven, soon ended his delight
And tortures him now more, the more he sees
Of pleasure not for him ordained; then soon   470
Fierce hate he recollects and all his thoughts
Of mischief, gratulating, thus excites:
    "Thoughts, whither have ye led me? with what
        sweet
Compulsion thus transported to forget
What hither brought us? hate, not love, nor hope   475
Of Paradise for Hell, hope here to taste
Of pleasure, but all pleasure to destroy,
Save what is in destroying; other joy
To me is lost. Then let me not let pass
Occasion which now smiles: behold alone   480
The woman, opportune to all attempts,
Her husband, for I view far round, not nigh,
Whose higher intellectual more I shun
And strength, of courage haughty and of limb
Heroic built, though of terrestrial mould;   485
Foe not informidable, exempt from wound,
I not; so much hath Hell debased and pain
Enfeebled me to what I was in Heaven.
She fair, divinely fair, fit love for gods,
Not terrible, though terror be in love   490
And beauty, not approached by stronger hate,
Hate stronger under show of love well feigned:
The way which to her ruin now I tend."
    So spake the enemy of mankind, enclosed
In serpent, inmate bad, and toward Eve   495
Addressed his way: not with indented wave
Prone on the ground, as since, but on his rear,
Circular base of rising folds, that towered

Fold above fold, a surging maze; his head
Crested aloft and carbuncle his eyes;   500
With burnished neck of verdant gold, erect
Amidst his circling spires, that on the grass
Floated redundant. Pleasing was his shape
And lovely; never since of serpent kind
Lovelier: not those that in Illyria changed,   505
Hermione and Cadmus, or the god
In Epidaurus; nor to which transformed
Ammonian Jove or Capitoline was seen,
He with Olympias, this with her who bore
Scipio, the highth of Rome. With tract oblique   510
At first, as one who sought access but feared
To interrupt, sidelong he works his way.
As when a ship by skilful steersman wrought
Nigh river's mouth or foreland, where the wind
Veers oft, as oft so steers and shifts her sail: 515
So varied he and of his tortuous train
Curled many a wanton wreath in sight of Eve
To lure her eye; she, busied, heard the sound
Of rustling leaves, but minded not, as used
To such disport before her through the field,   520
From every beast, more duteous at her call
Than at Circean call the herd disguised.
He, bolder now, uncalled before her stood
But as in gaze admiring. Oft he bowed
His turret crest and sleek enamelled neck,   525
Fawning, and licked the ground whereon she trod.
His gentle dumb expression turned at length
The eye of Eve to mark his play; he, glad
Of her attention gained, with serpent-tongue
Organic or impulse of vocal air,   530

His fraudulent temptation thus began:
  "Wonder not, sovran mistress, if perhaps
Thou canst, who art sole wonder; much less arm
Thy looks, the heaven of mildness, with disdain,
Displeased that I approach thee thus and gaze   535
Insatiate, I thus single, nor have feared
Thy awful brow, more awful thus retired.
Fairest resemblance of thy maker fair,
Thee all things living gaze on, all things thine
By gift, and thy celestial beauty adore,   540
With ravishment beheld: there best beheld
Where universally admired; but here
In this enclosure wild, these beasts among,
Beholders rude and shallow to discern
Half what in thee is fair, one man except,   545
Who sees thee? (and what is one?) who shouldst be
    seen
A goddess among gods, adored and served
By angels numberless, thy daily train."
  So glozed the tempter and his proem tuned.
Into the heart of Eve his words made way,   550
Though at the voice much marvelling; at length,
Not unamazed, she thus in answer spake:
  "What may this mean? language of man pronounced
By tongue of brute and human sense expressed!
The first at least of these I thought denied   555
To beasts, whom God on their creation-day
Created mute to all articulate sound;
The latter I demur, for in their looks
Much reason, and in their actions, oft appears.
Thee, serpent, subtlest beast of all the field   560
I knew, but not with human voice endued;

Redouble then this miracle and say,
How cam'st thou speakable of mute and how
To me so friendly grown above the rest
Of brutal kind, that daily are in sight: 565
Say, for such wonder claims attention due."
    To whom the guileful tempter thus replied:
"Empress of this fair world, resplendent Eve,
Easy to me it is to tell thee all
What thou command'st and right thou shouldst be
    obey'd.   570
I was at first as other beasts that graze
The trodden herb, of abject thoughts and low,
As was my food, nor aught but food discerned
Or sex and apprehended nothing high;
Till on a day, roving the field, I chanced   575
A goodly tree far distant to behold,
Loaden with fruit of fairest colours mixed,
Ruddy and gold. I nearer drew to gaze;
When from the boughs a savoury odour blown,
Grateful to appetite, more pleased my sense   580
Than smell of sweetest fennel or the teats
Of ewe or goat dropping with milk at even,
Unsucked of lamb or kid, that tend their play.
To satisfy the sharp desire I had
Of tasting those fair apples, I resolved   585
Not to defer; hunger and thirst at once,
Powerful persuaders, quickened at the scent
Of that alluring fruit, urged me so keen.
About the mossy trunk I wound me soon;
For, high from ground, the branches would
    require   590
Thy utmost reach or Adam's: round the tree

All other beasts that saw, with like desire
Longing and envying stood but could not reach.
Amid the tree now got, where plenty hung
Tempting so nigh, to pluck and eat my fill   595
I spared not; for such pleasure till that hour
At feed or fountain never had I found.
Sated at length, ere long I might perceive
Strange alteration in me, to degree
Of reason in my inward powers; and speech   600
Wanted not long, though to this shape retained.
Thenceforth to speculations high or deep
I turned my thoughts and with capacious mind
Considered all things visible in Heaven,
Or Earth, or middle, all things fair and good: 605
But all that fair and good in thy divine
Semblance and in thy beauty's heavenly ray
United I beheld; no fair to thine
Equivalent or second, which compelled
Me thus, though importune perhaps, to come   610
And gaze, and worship thee of right declared
Sovran of creatures, universal dame.
     So talked the spirited sly snake; and Eve,
Yet more amazed, unwary thus replied:
     "Serpent, thy overpraising leaves in doubt   615
The virtue of that fruit, in thee first proved.
But say, where grows the tree? from hence how far?
For many are the trees of God that grow
In Paradise, and various, yet unknown
To us; in such abundance lies our choice,   620
As leaves a greater store of fruit untouched,
Still hanging incorruptible, till men
Grow up to their provision and more hands

Help to disburden nature of her birth."
   To whom the wily adder, blithe and glad: 625
   "Empress, the way is ready and not long:
Beyond a row of myrtles, on a flat,
Fast by a fountain, one small thicket past
Of blowing myrrh and balm. If thou accept
My conduct, I can bring thee thither soon."   630
   "Lead then," said Eve. He leading swiftly rolled
In tangles and made intricate seem straight,
To mischief swift. Hope elevates, and joy
Brightens his crest. As when a wandering fire,
Compact of unctuous vapour, which the night   635
Condenses and the cold environs round,
Kindled through agitation to a flame
(Which oft, they say, some evil spirit attends),
Hovering and blazing with delusive light,
Misleads the amazed night-wanderer from his way 640
To bogs and mires, and oft through pond or pool,
There swallowed up and lost, from succour far:
So glistered the dire snake and into fraud
Led Eve, our credulous mother, to the tree
Of prohibition, root of all our woe.   645
Which when she saw, this to her guide she spake:
   "Serpent, we might have spared our coming hither,
Fruitless to me, though fruit be here to excess;
The credit of whose virtue rest with thee—
Wondrous indeed, if cause of such effects!   650
But of this tree we may not taste nor touch;
God so commanded and left that command
Sole daughter of his voice: the rest, we live
Law to ourselves; our reason is our law."
   To whom the tempter guilefully replied: 655

"Indeed? Hath God then said that of the fruit
Of all these garden-trees ye shall not eat,
Yet lords declared of all in Earth or air?'

    To whom thus Eve, yet sinless: "Of the fruit
Of each tree in the garden we may eat;   660
But of the fruit of this fair tree amidst
The garden God hath said, 'Ye shall not eat
Thereof nor shall ye touch it, lest ye die.'"

    She scarce had said, though brief, when now more
        bold
The tempter, but with show of zeal and love   665
To man and indignation at his wrong,
New part puts on and, as to passion moved,
Fluctuates disturbed, yet comely and in act
Raised, as of some great matter to begin.
As when of old some orator renowned   670
In Athens or free Rome, where eloquence
Flourished, since mute, to some great cause addressed,
Stood in himself collected, while each part,
Motion, each act, won audience ere the tongue,
Sometimes in highth began, as no delay   675
Of preface brooking through his zeal of right:
So standing, moving, or to highth upgrown,
The tempter, all impassioned, thus began:

    "O sacred, wise, and wisdom-giving plant,
Mother of science, now I feel thy power   680
Within me clear, not only to discern
Things in their causes but to trace the ways
Of highest agents, deemed however wise.
Queen of this universe, do not believe
Those rigid threats of death. Ye shall not die: 685
How should ye? by the fruit? it gives you life

To knowledge; by the threatener? look on me,
Me who have touched and tasted yet both live
And life more perfect have attained than fate
Meant me, by ventring higher than my lot. 690
Shall that be shut to man which to the beast
Is open? or will God incense his ire
For such a petty trespass and not praise
Rather your dauntless virtue, whom the pain
Of death denounced, whatever thing death be, 695
Deterred not from achieving what might lead
To happier life, knowledge of good and evil?
Of good, how just? of evil, if what is evil
Be real, why not known, since easier shunned?
God therefore cannot hurt ye and be just: 700
Not just, not God; not feared then, nor obeyed.
Your fear itself of death removes the fear.
Why then was this forbid? Why but to awe,
Why but to keep ye low and ignorant,
His worshippers? He knows that in the day 705
Ye eat thereof, your eyes, that seem so clear
Yet are but dim, shall perfectly be then
Opened and cleared, and ye shall be as gods,
Knowing both good and evil, as they know.
That ye should be as gods, since I as man, 710
Internal man, is but proportion meet:
I, of brute, human; ye, of human, gods.
So yet shall die perhaps, but putting off
Human, to put on gods: death to be wished,
Though threatened, which no worse than this can
    bring! 715
And what are gods, that man may not become
As they, participating godlike food?

The gods are first and that advantage use
On our belief that all from them proceeds.
I question it; for this fair Earth I see,   720
Warmed by the sun, producing every kind,
Them nothing: if they all things, who enclosed
Knowledge of good and evil in this tree,
That whoso eats thereof forthwith attains
Wisdom without their leave? and wherein lies   725
The offence, that man should thus attain to know?
What can your knowledge hurt him, or this tree
Impart against his will, if all be his?
Or is it envy? and can envy dwell
In heavenly breasts? These, these and many more   730
Causes import your need of this fair fruit.
Goddess humane, reach then and freely taste."
    He ended, and his words, replete with guile,
Into her heart too easy entrance won.
Fixed on the fruit she gazed, which to behold   735
Might tempt alone, and in her ears the sound
Yet rung of his persuasive words, impregned
With reason, to her seeming, and with truth.
Meanwhile the hour of noon drew on and waked
An eager appetite, raised by the smell   740
So savoury of that fruit, which with desire,
Inclinable now grown to touch or taste,
Solicited her longing eye; yet first,
Pausing a while, thus to herself she mused:
    "Great are thy virtues, doubtless, best of fruits, 745
Though kept from man, and worthy to be admired,
Whose taste, too long forborne, at first assay
Gave elocution to the mute and taught
The tongue not made for speech to speak thy praise.

Thy praise he also who forbids thy use   750
Conceals not from us, naming thee the Tree
Of Knowledge, knowledge both of good and evil:
Forbid us then to taste; but his forbidding
Commends thee more, while it infers the good
By thee communicated and our want;   755
For good unknown sure is not had, or had
And yet unknown, is as not had at all.
In plain then, what forbids he but to know?
Forbids us good, forbids us to be wise.
Such prohibitions bind not. But if death   760
Bind us with after-bands, what profits then
Our inward freedom? In the day we eat
Of this fair fruit, our doom is, we shall die.
How dies the serpent? He hath eaten and lives
And knows and speaks and reasons and discerns, 765
Irrational till then. For us alone
Was death invented? or to us denied
This intellectual food, for beasts reserved?
For beasts it seems; yet that one beast which first
Hath tasted envies not but brings with joy   770
The good befallen him, author unsuspect,
Friendly to man, far from deceit or guile.
What fear I then? rather, what know to fear
Under this ignorance of good and evil,
Of God or death, of law or penalty?   775
Here grows the cure of all, this fruit divine,
Fair to the eye, inviting to the taste,
Of virtue to make wise: what hinders then
To reach and feed at once both body and mind?"
   So saying, her rash hand in evil hour   780
Forth reaching to the fruit, she plucked, she eat.

Earth felt the wound, and Nature from her seat,
Sighing through all her works, gave signs of woe
That all was lost. Back to the thicket slunk
The guilty serpent and well might, for Eve, 785
Intent now only on her taste, naught else
Regarded; such delight till then, as seemed,
In fruit she never tasted, whether true
Or fancied so through expectation high
Of knowledge; nor was godhead from her
    thought. 790
Greedily she ingorged without restraint,
And knew not eating death. Satiate at length
And hightened as with wine, jocund and boon,
Thus to herself she pleasingly began:
  "O sovran, virtuous, precious of all trees 795
In Paradise, of operation blest
To sapience, hitherto obscured, infamed,
And thy fair fruit let hang, as to no end
Created! but henceforth my early care,
Not without song, each morning, and due praise, 800
Shall tend thee and the fertile burden ease
Of thy full branches, offered free to all;
Till, dieted by thee, I grow mature
In knowledge, as the gods who all things know;
Though others envy what they cannot give— 805
For, had the gift been theirs, it had not here
Thus grown. Experience, next to thee I owe,
Best guide; not following thee, I had remained
In ignorance: thou open'st wisdom's way,
And giv'st access, though secret she retire. 810
And I perhaps am secret; Heaven is high,
High and remote to see from thence distinct

Each thing on Earth; and other care perhaps
May have diverted from continual watch
Our great Forbidder, safe with all his spies   815
About him. But to Adam in what sort
Shall I appear? Shall I to him make known
As yet my change and give him to partake
Full happiness with me; or rather not,
But keep the odds of knowledge in my power   820
Without copartner? so to add what wants
In female sex, the more to draw his love,
And render me more equal and perhaps,
A thing not undesirable, sometime
Superior; for, inferior, who is free?   825
This may be well: but what if God have seen,
And death ensue? then I shall be no more,
And Adam, wedded to another Eve,
Shall live with her enjoying, I extinct.
A death to think! Confirmed then I resolve: 830
Adam shall share with me in bliss or woe.
So dear I love him, that with him all deaths
I could endure, without him live no life."

    So saying, from the tree her step she turned,
But first low reverence done, as to the power   835
That dwelt within, whose presence had infused
Into the plant sciential sap, derived
From nectar, drink of gods. Adam the while,
Waiting desirous her return, had wove
Of choicest flowers a garland to adorn   840
Her tresses and her rural labours crown,
As reapers oft are wont their harvest queen.
Great joy he promised to his thoughts and new
Solace in her return, so long delayed:

Yet oft his heart, divine of something ill,   845
Misgave him; he the faltering measure felt
And forth to meet her went, the way she took
That morn when first they parted. By the Tree
Of Knowledge he must pass: there he her met
Scarce from the tree returning; in her hand   850
A bough of fairest fruit, that downy smiled,
New gathered, and ambrosial smell diffused.
To him she hasted; in her face excuse
Came prologue and apology to prompt,
Which, with bland words at will, she thus
    addressed: 855
"Hast thou not wondered, Adam, at my stay?
Thee I have missed, and thought it long, deprived
Thy presence: agony of love till now
Not felt, nor shall be twice; for never more
Mean I to try, what rash untried I sought,   860
The pain of absence from thy sight. But strange
Hath been the cause and wonderful to hear.
This tree is not, as we are told, a tree
Of danger, tasted, nor to evil unknown
Opening the way, but of divine effect   865
To open eyes and make them gods who taste;
And hath been tasted such. The serpent wise,
Or not restrained as we or not obeying,
Hath eaten of the fruit and is become,
Not dead, as we are threatened, but thenceforth   870
Endued with human voice and human sense,
Reasoning to admiration, and with me,
Persuasively hath so prevailed, that I
Have also tasted and have also found
The effects to correspond: opener mine eyes,   875

Dim erst, dilated spirits, ampler heart,
And growing up to godhead; which for thee
Chiefly I sought, without thee can despise.
For bliss, as thou hast part, to me is bliss;
Tedious, unshared with thee, and odious soon.   880
Thou therefore also taste, that equal lot
May join us, equal joy, as equal love;
Lest, thou not tasting, different degree
Disjoin us, and I then too late renounce
Deity for thee, when fate will not permit."   885
    Thus Eve with countenance blithe her story told;
But in her cheek distemper flushing glowed.
On the other side, Adam, soon as he heard
The fatal trespass done by Eve, amazed,
Astonied stood and blank, while horror chill   890
Ran through his veins and all his joints relaxed;
From his slack hand the garland wreathed for Eve
Down dropt and all the faded roses shed.
Speechless he stood and pale, till thus at length
First to himself he inward silence broke: 895
    "O fairest of creation, last and best
Of all God's works, creature in whom excelled
Whatever can to sight or thought be formed,
Holy, divine, good, amiable, or sweet,
How art thou lost! how on a sudden lost,   900
Defaced, deflowered, and now to death devote!
Rather, how hast thou yielded to transgress
The strict forbiddance, now to violate
The sacred fruit forbidden? Some cursed fraud
Of enemy hath beguiled thee, yet unknown,   905
And me with thee hath ruined; for with thee
Certain my resolution is to die.

How can I live without thee? how forgo
Thy sweet converse and love so dearly joined,
To live again in these wild woods forlorn? 910
Should God create another Eve, and I
Another rib afford, yet loss of thee
Would never from my heart: no, no, I feel
The link of nature draw me; flesh of flesh,
Bone of my bone thou art, and from thy state 915
Mine never shall be parted, bliss or woe."

So having said, as one from sad dismay
Recomforted and after thoughts disturbed
Submitting to what seemed remediless,
Thus in calm mood his words to Eve he turned: 920
"Bold deed thou hast presumed, adventurous Eve,
And peril great provoked, who thus hast dared,
Had it been only coveting to eye
That sacred fruit, sacred to abstinence;
Much more to taste it, under ban to touch. 925
But past who can recall, or done undo?
Not God omnipotent, nor fate. Yet so
Perhaps thou shalt not die; perhaps the fact
Is not so heinous now, foretasted fruit,
Profaned first by the Serpent, by him first 930
Made common and unhallowed ere our taste,
Nor yet on him found deadly. He yet lives,
Lives, as thou saidst, and gains to live, as man,
Higher degree of life: inducement strong
To us, as likely, tasting, to attain 935
Proportional ascent; which cannot be
But to be gods or angels, demi-gods.
Nor can I think that God, creator wise,
Though threatening, will in earnest so destroy

Us his prime creatures, dignified so high, 940
Set over all his works, which in our fall,
For us created, needs with us must fail,
Dependent made: so God shall uncreate,
Be frustrate, do, undo, and labour lose;
Not well conceived of God, who, though his power 945
Creation could repeat, yet would be loth
Us to abolish, lest the adversary
Triumph and say: 'Fickle their state whom God
Most favours; who can please him long? Me first
He ruined, now mankind; whom will he next?' 950
Matter of scorn not to be given the foe.
However, I with thee have fixed my lot,
Certain to undergo like doom: if death
Consort with thee, death is to me as life;
So forcible within my heart I feel 955
The bond of nature draw me to my own,
My own in thee, for what thou art is mine.
Our state cannot be severed; we are one,
One flesh; to lose thee were to lose myself."

   So Adam, and thus Eve to him replied: 960
"O glorious trial of exceeding love,
Illustrious evidence, example high,
Engaging me to emulate; but, short
Of thy perfection, how shall I attain,
Adam? from whose dear side I boast me sprung 965
And gladly of our union hear thee speak,
One heart, one soul in both: whereof good proof
This day affords, declaring thee resolved,
Rather than death, or aught than death more dread,
Shall separate us, linked in love so dear, 970
To undergo with me one guilt, one crime,

If any be, of tasting this fair fruit;
Whose virtue (for of good still good proceeds,
Direct or by occasion) hath presented
This happy trial of thy love, which else   975
So eminently never had been known.
Were it I thought death menaced would ensue
This my attempt, I would sustain alone
The worst and not persuade thee, rather die
Deserted than oblige thee with a fact   980
Pernicious to thy peace, chiefly assured
Remarkably so late of thy so true,
So faithful love unequalled. But I feel
Far otherwise the event: not death, but life
Augmented, opened eyes, new hopes, new joys,   985
Taste so divine, that what of sweet before
Hath touched my sense flat seems to this and harsh.
On my experience, Adam, freely taste
And fear of death deliver to the winds."
    So saying, she embraced him and for joy   990
Tenderly wept, much won that he his love
Had so ennobled as of choice to incur
Divine displeasure for her sake or death.
In recompense (for such compliance bad
Such recompense best merits) from the bough   995
She gave him of that fair enticing fruit
With liberal hand; he scrupled not to eat.
Against his better knowledge, not deceived
But fondly overcome with female charm.
Earth trembled from her entrails, as again   1000
In pangs, and nature gave a second groan;
Sky loured, and, muttering thunder, some sad drops
Wept at completing of the mortal sin

Original; while Adam took no thought,
Eating his fill, nor Eve to iterate   1005
Her former trespass feared, the more to soothe
Him with her loved society; that now,
As with new wine intoxicated both,
They swim in mirth and fancy that they feel
Divinity within them breeding wings   1010
Wherewith to scorn the earth. But that false fruit
Far other operation first displayed,
Carnal desire inflaming: he on Eve
Began to cast lascivious eyes; she him
As wantonly repaid; in lust they burn,   1015
Till Adam thus 'gan Eve to dalliance move:
    "Eve, now I see thou art exact of taste
And elegant, of sapience no small part;
Since to each meaning savour we apply
And palate call judicious. I the praise   1020
Yield thee, so well this day thou hast purveyed.
Much pleasure we have lost, while we abstained
From this delightful fruit nor known till now
True relish, tasting; if such pleasure be
In things to us forbidden, it might be wished   1025
For this one tree had been forbidden ten.
But come; so well refreshed, now let us play,
As meet is, after such delicious fare:
For never did thy beauty, since the day
I saw thee first and wedded thee, adorned   1030
With all perfections, so inflame my sense
With ardour to enjoy thee, fairer now
Than ever, bounty of this virtuous tree."
    So said he and forbore not glance or toy
Of amorous intent, well understood   1035

Of Eve, whose eye darted contagious fire.
Her hand he seized and to a shady bank,
Thick overhead with verdant roof embowered,
He led her nothing loth; flowers were the couch,
Pansies and violets and asphodel,   1040
And hyacinth, Earth's freshest, softest lap.
There they their fill of love and love's disport
Took largely, of their mutual guilt the seal,
The solace of their sin, till dewy sleep
Oppressed them, wearied with their amorous
    play.   1045
  Soon as the force of that fallacious fruit,
That with exhilarating vapour bland
About their spirits had played and inmost powers
Made err, was now exhaled, and grosser sleep,
Bred of unkindly fumes, with conscious dreams   1050
Encumbered, now had left them, up they rose
As from unrest, and, each the other viewing,
Soon found their eyes how opened, and their minds
How darkened. Innocence, that as a veil
Had shadowed them from knowing ill, was gone;   1055
Just confidence, and native righteousness,
And honour, from about them, naked left
To guilty Shame: he covered, but his robe
Uncovered more. So rose the Danite strong,
Herculean Samson, from the harlot-lap   1060
Of Philistean Dalilah and waked
Shorn of his strength; they destitute and bare
Of all their virtue. Silent and in face
Confounded, long they sat, as strucken mute;
Till Adam, though not less than Eve abashed,   1065
At length gave utterance to these words constrained:

"O Eve, in evil hour thou didst give ear
To that false worm, of whomsoever taught
To counterfeit man's voice, true in our fall,
False in our promised rising; since our eyes   1070
Opened we find indeed and find we know
Both good and evil, good lost and evil got:
Bad fruit of knowledge, if this be to know,
Which leaves us naked thus, of honour void,
Of innocence, of faith, of purity,   1075
Our wonted ornaments now soiled and stained,
And in our faces evident the signs
Of foul concupiscence; whence evil store,
Even shame, the last of evils; of the first
Be sure then. How shall I behold the face   1080
Henceforth of god or angel, erst with joy
And rapture so oft beheld? those heavenly shapes
Will dazzle now this earthly with their blaze
Insufferably bright. Oh, might I here
In solitude live savage, in some glade   1085
Obscured, where highest woods, impenetrable
To star or sunlight, spread their umbrage broad,
And brown as evening! Cover me, ye pines;
Ye cedars, with innumerable boughs
Hide me, where I may never see them more!   1090
But let us now, as in bad plight, devise
What best may for the present serve to hide
The parts of each from other that seem most
To shame obnoxious and unseemliest seen;
Some tree, whose broad smooth leaves together
          sewed   1095
And girded on our loins, may cover round
Those middle parts, that this new comer, Shame,

There sit not and reproach us as unclean."
   So counselled he, and both together went
Into the thickest wood; there soon they chose   1100
The fig-tree—not that kind for fruit renowned,
But such as at this day, to Indians known,
In Malabar or Decan spreads her arms
Branching so broad and long that in the ground
The bended twigs take root, and daughters grow 1105
About the mother tree, a pillared shade
High overarched, and echoing walks between:
There oft the Indian herdsman, shunning heat,
Shelters in cool and tends his pasturing herds
At loop-holes cut through thickest shade. Those
     leaves   1110
They gathered, broad as Amazonian targe,
And with what skill they had together sewed,
To gird their waist; vain covering, if to hide
Their guilt and dreaded shame. Oh how unlike
To that first naked glory! Such of late   1115
Columbus found the American, so girt
With feathered cincture, naked else and wild
Among the trees on isles and woody shores.
Thus fenced, and, as they thought, their shame in part
Covered, but not at rest or ease of mind,   1120
They sat them down to weep; nor only tears
Rained at their eyes, but high winds worse within
Began to rise, high passions, anger, hate,
Mistrust, suspicion, discord, and shook sore
Their inward state of mind, calm region once   1125
And full of peace, now tost and turbulent:
For understanding ruled not, and the will
Heard not her lore, both in subjection now

To sensual appetite, who, from beneath
Usurping over sovran reason, claimed   1130
Superior sway. From thus distempered breast
Adam, estranged in look and altered style,
Speech intermitted thus to Eve renewed:
    "Would thou hadst hearkened to my words and
        stayed
With me, as I besought thee, when that strange 1135
Desire of wandering, this unhappy morn,
I know not whence possessed thee! we had then
Remained still happy, not, as now, despoiled
Of all our good, shamed, naked, miserable.
Let none henceforth seek needless cause to
        approve   1140
The faith they owe; when earnestly they seek
Such proof, conclude, they then begin to fail."
    To whom, soon moved with touch of blame, thus
        Eve:
"What words have passed thy lips, Adam severe!
Imput'st thou that to my default, or will   1145
Of wandering, as thou call'st it, which who knows
But might as ill have happened, thou being by,
Or to thyself perhaps? Hadst thou been there,
Or here the attempt, thou couldst not have discerned
Fraud in the serpent, speaking as he spake;   1150
No ground of enmity between us known,
Why he should mean me ill or seek to harm.
Was I to have never parted from thy side?
As good have grown there still, a lifeless rib.
Being as I am, why didst not thou, the head,   1155
Command me absolutely not to go,
Going into such danger, as thou saidst?

Too facile then, thou didst not much gainsay,
Nay, didst permit, approve, and fair dismiss.
Hadst thou been firm and fixed in thy dissent,   1160
Neither had I transgressed, nor thou with me."
     To whom, then first incensed, Adam replied:
"Is this the love, is this the recompense
Of mine to thee, ingrateful Eve, expressed
Immutable when thou wert lost, not I,   1165
Who might have lived and joyed immortal bliss,
Yet willingly chose rather death with thee?
And am I now upbraided as the cause
Of thy transgressing? not enough severe,
It seems, in thy restraint! What could I more?   1170
I warned thee, I admonished thee, foretold
The danger and the lurking enemy
That lay in wait; beyond this had been force,
And force upon free will hath here no place.
But confidence then bore thee on, secure   1175
Either to meet no danger or to find
Matter of glorious trial; and perhaps
I also erred in overmuch admiring
What seemed in thee so perfect, that I thought
No evil durst attempt thee: but I rue   1180
That error now, which is become my crime,
And thou the accuser. Thus it shall befall
Him who, to worth in women overtrusting,
Lets her will rule: restraint she will not brook;
And, left to herself, if evil thence ensue,   1185
She first his weak indulgence will accuse."
     Thus they in mutual accusation spent
The fruitless hours, but neither self-condemning;
And of their vain contest appeared no end.

PARADISE LOST

Book X

Meanwhile the heinous and despiteful act
Of Satan done in Paradise, and how
He, in the serpent, had perverted Eve,
Her husband she, to taste the fatal fruit,
Was known in Heaven; for what can scape the eye   5
Of God all-seeing or deceive his heart
Omniscient? who, in all things wise and just,
Hindered not Satan to attempt the mind
Of man, with strength entire and free will armed,
Complete to have discovered and repulsed   10
Whatever wiles of foe or seeming friend.
For still they knew and ought to have still remembered
The high injunction not to taste that fruit,
Whoever tempted; which they not obeying
Incurred (what could they less?) the penalty   15
And, manifold in sin, deserved to fall.

    Up into Heaven from Paradise in haste
The angelic guards ascended, mute and sad
For man; for of his state by this they knew,
Much wondering how the subtle fiend had stolen   20
Entrance unseen. Soon as the unwelcome news
From Earth arrived at Heaven-gate, displeased
All were who heard; dim sadness did not spare

That time celestial visages, yet, mixed
With pity, violated not their bliss.   25
About the new-arrived in multitudes
The ethereal people ran, to hear and know
How all befell. They towards the throne supreme,
Accountable, made haste, to make appear
With righteous plea their utmost vigilance,   30
And easily approved; when the Most High
Eternal Father, from his secret cloud
Amidst, in thunder uttered thus his voice:
    "Assembled angels and ye powers returned
From unsuccessful charge, be not dismayed   35
Nor troubled at these tidings from the Earth,
Which your sincerest care could not prevent,
Foretold so lately what would come to pass,
When first this tempter crossed the gulf from Hell.
I told ye then he should prevail and speed   40
On his bad errand: man should be seduced
And flattered out of all, believing lies
Against his maker; no decree of mine
Concurring to necessitate his fall
Or touch with lightest moment of impulse   45
His free will, to her own inclining left
In even scale. But fallen he is; and now
What rests, but that the mortal sentence pass
On his transgression, death denounced that day?
Which he presumes already vain and void,   50
Because not yet inflicted, as he feared,
By some immediate stroke; but soon shall find
Forbearance no acquittance ere day end:
Justice shall not return, as bounty scorned.
But whom send I to judge them? whom but thee,   55

Vicegerent Son? to thee I have transferred
All judgment, whether in Heaven or Earth or Hell.
Easy it may be seen that I intend
Mercy colleague with justice, sending thee,
Man's friend, his mediator, his designed   60
Both ransom and redeemer voluntary
And destined man himself to judge man fallen."
　　So spake the Father; and, unfolding bright
Toward the right hand his glory, on the Son
Blazed forth unclouded deity; he full   65
Resplendent all his Father manifest
Expressed and thus divinely answered mild:
　　"Father eternal, thine is to decree,
Mine both in Heaven and Earth to do thy will
Supreme, that thou in me, thy son beloved,   70
May'st ever rest well pleased. I go to judge
On Earth these thy transgressors: but thou know'st,
Whoever judged, the worst on me must light,
When time shall be; for so I undertook
Before thee, and, not repenting, this obtain   75
Of right, that I may mitigate their doom
On me derived. Yet I shall temper so
Justice with mercy, as may illustrate most
Them fully satisfied, and thee appease.
Attendance none shall need nor train, where none   80
Are to behold the judgment but the judged,
Those two; the third best absent is condemned,
Convict by flight and rebel to all law:
Conviction to the serpent none belongs."
　　Thus saying, from his radiant seat he rose   85
Of high collateral glory; him Thrones and Powers,
Princedoms and Dominations ministrant

Accompanied to Heaven-gate, from whence
Eden and all the coast in prospect lay.
Down he descended straight; the speed of gods   90
Time counts not, though with swiftest minutes
    winged.
  Now was the sun in western cadence low
From noon, and gentle airs due at their hour
To fan the Earth now waked and usher in
The evening cool, when he, from wrath more cool, 95
Came, the mild judge and intercessor both,
To sentence man. The voice of God they heard
Now walking in the garden, by soft winds
Brought to their ears, while day declined; they heard,
And from his presence hid themselves among   100
The thickest trees, both man and wife, till God,
Approaching, thus to Adam called aloud:
  "Where art thou, Adam, wont with joy to meet
My coming seen far off? I miss thee here,
Not pleased, thus entertained with solitude,   105
Where obvious duty erewhile appeared unsought.
Or come I less conspicuous or what change
Absents thee or what chance detains? Come forth."
  He came, and with him Eve, more loth, though
    first
To offend, discountenanced both and discomposed; 110
Love was not in their looks either to God
Or to each other, but apparent guilt
And shame and perturbation and despair,
Anger and obstinacy and hate and guile.
Whence Adam, faltering long, thus answered
    brief: 115
  "I heard thee in the garden and of thy voice

Afraid, being naked, hid myself." To whom
The gracious judge without revile replied:
   "My voice thou oft hast heard and hast not feared,
But still rejoiced; how is it now become   120
So dreadful to thee? That thou art naked, who
Hath told thee? Hast thou eaten of the tree
Whereof I gave thee charge thou shouldst not eat?"
   To whom thus Adam, sore beset, replied:
   "O Heaven! in evil strait this day I stand   125
Before my judge: either to undergo
Myself the total crime or to accuse
My other self, the partner of my life;
Whose failing, while her faith to me remains,
I should conceal and not expose to blame   130
By my complaint; but strict necessity
Subdues me and calamitous constraint,
Lest on my head both sin and punishment,
However insupportable, be all
Devolved; though should I hold my peace, yet
     thou   135
Wouldst easily detect what I conceal.
This woman, whom thou mad'st to be my help,
And gav'st me as thy perfect gift, so good,
So fit, so acceptable, so divine,
That from her hand I could suspect no ill,   140
And what she did, whatever in itself,
Her doing seemed to justify the deed—
She gave me of the tree, and I did eat."
   To whom the Sovran Presence thus replied:
   "Was she thy God, that her thou didst obey   145
Before his voice? or was she made thy guide,
Superior or but equal, that to her

Thou didst resign thy manhood and the place
Wherein God set thee above her, made of thee   150
And for thee, whose perfection far excelled
Hers in all real dignity? Adorned
She was indeed and lovely, to attract
Thy love, not thy subjection; and her gifts
Were such as under government well seemed,   155
Unseemly to bear rule; which was thy part
And person, hadst thou known thyself aright."

   So having said, he thus to Eve in few:
"Say, woman, what is this which thou hast done?"

   To whom sad Eve, with shame nigh overwhelmed,
Confessing soon yet not before her judge   160
Bold or loquacious, thus abashed replied:
"The serpent me beguiled, and I did eat."

   Which when the Lord God heard, without delay
To judgment he proceeded on the accused
Serpent, though brute unable to transfer   165
The guilt on him who made him instrument
Of mischief and polluted from the end
Of his creation; justly then accursed,
As vitiated in nature. More to know
Concerned not man (since he no further knew),   170
Nor altered his offence; yet God at last
To Satan, first in sin, his doom applied,
Though in mysterious terms, judged as then best;
And on the Serpent thus his curse let fall:

   "Because thou hast done this, thou art accursed 175
Above all cattle, each beast of the field;
Upon thy belly grovelling thou shalt go
And dust shalt eat all the days of thy life.
Between thee and the woman I will put

Enmity, and between thine and her seed;   180
Her seed shall bruise thy head, thou bruise his heel."
  So spake this oracle, then verified
When Jesus, son of Mary, second Eve,
Saw Satan fall like lightning down from Heaven,
Prince of the air; then, rising from his grave,   185
Spoiled principalities and powers, triumphed
In open show, and with ascension bright
Captivity led captive through the air,
The realm itself of Satan long usurped,
Whom he shall tread at last under our feet;   190
Even he who now foretold his fatal bruise,
And to the Woman thus his sentence turned:
  "Thy sorrow I will greatly multiply
By thy conception; children thou shalt bring
In sorrow forth; and to thy husband's will   195
Thine shall submit; he over thee shall rule."
  On Adam last thus judgment he pronounced:
"Because thou hast hearkened to the voice of thy
        wife
And eaten of the tree, concerning which
I charged thee, saying, 'Thou shalt not eat
        thereof,'   200
Curs'd is the ground for thy sake; thou in sorrow
Shalt eat thereof all the days of thy life;
Thorns also and thistles it shall bring thee forth
Unbid; and thou shalt eat the herb of the field;
In the sweat of thy face shalt thou eat bread,   205
Till thou return unto the ground; for thou
Out of the ground wast taken: know thy birth,
For dust thou art and shalt to dust return."
  So judged he man, both judge and saviour sent,

And the instant stroke of death, denounced that
    day,   210
Removed far off; then, pitying how they stood
Before him naked to the air, that now
Must suffer change, disdained not to begin
Thenceforth the form of servant to assume:
As when he washed his servants' feet, so now,   215
As father of his family, he clad
Their nakedness with skins of beasts, or slain
Or as the snake with youthful coat repaid;
And thought not much to clothe his enemies.
Nor he their outward only with the skins   220
Of beasts, but inward nakedness, much more
Opprobrious, with his robe of righteousness
Arraying, covered from his Father's sight.
To him with swift ascent he up returned,
Into his blissful bosom reassumed   225
In glory as of old; to him appeased
All, though all-knowing, what had passed with man
Recounted, mixing intercession sweet.
    Meanwhile, ere thus was sinned and judged on
    Earth,
Within the gates of Hell sat Sin and Death,   230
In counterview within the gates, that now
Stood open wide, belching outrageous flame
Far into Chaos, since the fiend passed through,
Sin opening; who thus now to Death began:
    "O son, why sit we here each other viewing   235
Idly, while Satan, our great author, thrives
In other worlds and happier seat provides
For us, his offspring dear? It cannot be
But that success attends him; if mishap,

Ere this he had returned, with fury driven   240
By his avengers, since no place like this
Can fit his punishment or their revenge.
Methinks I feel new strength within me rise,
Wings growing, and dominion given me large
Beyond this deep, whatever draws me on,   245
Or sympathy or some connatural force,
Powerful at greatest distance to unite
With secret amity things of like kind
By secretest conveyance. Thou, my shade
Inseparable, must with me along;   250
For Death from Sin no power can separate.
But, lest the difficulty of passing back
Stay his return perhaps over this gulf
Impassable, impervious, let us try
Adventurous work, yet to thy power and mine   255
Not unagreeable, to found a path
Over this main from Hell to that new world
Where Satan now prevails; a monument
Of merit high to all the infernal host,
Easing their passage hence, for intercourse   260
Or transmigration, as their lot shall lead.
Nor can I miss the way, so strongly drawn
By this new-felt attraction and instinct."
    Whom thus the meagre shadow answered soon:
"Go whither fate and inclination strong   265
Leads thee: I shall not lag behind nor err
The way, thou leading; such a scent I draw
Of carnage, prey innumerable, and taste
The savour of death from all things there that live,
Nor shall I to the work thou enterprisest   270
Be wanting but afford thee equal aid."

So saying, with delight he snuffed the smell
Of mortal change on Earth. As when a flock
Of ravenous fowl, though many a league remote,
Against the day of battle, to a field   275
Where armies lie encamped, come flying, lured
With scent of living carcases designed   marked
For death the following day in bloody fight:
So scented the grim feature and upturned   form
His nostril wide into the murky air,   280
Sagacious of his quarry from so far.
Then both from out Hell-gates into the waste
Wide anarchy of Chaos damp and dark
Flew diverse, and with power (their power was
       great),
Hovering upon the waters, what they met   285
Solid or slimy, as in raging sea
Tossed up and down, together crowded drove,
From each side shoaling, towards the mouth of Hell;
As when two polar winds, blowing adverse
Upon the Cronian sea, together drive   290
Mountains of ice, that stop the imagined way
Beyond Petsora eastward to the rich
Cathaian coast. The aggregated soil
Death with his mace petrific, cold and dry,
As with a trident smote and fixed as firm   295
As Delos, floating once: the rest his look
Bound with Gorgonian rigour not to move
And with asphaltic slime; broad as the gate
Deep to the roots of Hell the gathered beach
They fastened and the mole immense wrought on   300
Over the foaming deep high-arched, a bridge
Of length prodigious, joining to the wall

Margin annotations:
Able to scent
In different directions
Heaping into a bank
Arctic
North Sea Psye.
China + Cathay conquered. rus = N. China
Bituminous
from opposite directions
Gulf in Arctic sea (W/E) by Nova Zembl
Gorgon kill by Persee
into the Hell of universe.

Tufts found Delos in sea bed — bird of
Myrtle + Drava.

Immovable of this now fenceless world, *defenceless.*
Forfeit to Death; from hence a passage broad,
Smooth, easy, inoffensive, down to Hell. *unobstructed.* 305
So, if great things to small may be compared,
Xerxes, the liberty of Greece to yoke,
From Susa, his Memnonian palace high,
Came to the sea and, over Hellespont
Bridging his way, Europe with Asia joined 310
And scourged with many a stroke the indignant waves.
Now had they brought the work by wondrous art
Pontifical, a ridge of pendent rock,
Over the vexed abyss, following the track
Of Satan, to the self-same place where he 315
First lighted from his wing and landed safe
From out of Chaos, to the outside bare
Of this round world. With pins of adamant
And chains they made all fast, too fast they made
And durable; and now in little space 320
The confines met of empyrean Heaven
And of this world and on the left hand Hell
With long reach interposed; three several ways
In sight to each of these three places led.
And now their way to Earth they had descried, 325
To Paradise first tending, when, behold!
Satan, in likeness of an angel bright,
Betwixt the Centaur and the Scorpion steering
His zenith, while the sun in Aries rose.
Disguised he came; but those his children dear 330
Their parent soon discerned, though in disguise.
He, after Eve seduced, unminded slunk
Into the wood fast by, and, changing shape
To observe the sequel, saw his guileful act

By Eve, though all unweeting, seconded   335
Upon her husband, saw their shame that sought
Vain covertures; but when he saw descend
The Son of God to judge them, terrified
He fled, not hoping to escape but shun
The present, fearing guilty what his wrath   340
Might suddenly inflict; that past, returned
By night, and listening where the hapless pair
Sat in their sad discourse and various plaint,
Thence gathered his own doom; which understood
Not instant but of future time, with joy   345
And tidings fraught, to Hell he now returned
And at the brink of Chaos, near the foot
Of this new wondrous pontifice, unhoped
Met who to meet him came, his offspring dear.
Great joy was at their meeting, and at sight   350
Of that stupendous bridge his joy increased.
Long he admiring stood, till Sin, his fair
Enchanting daughter, thus the silence broke:
  "O parent, these are thy magnific deeds,
Thy tropies, which thou view'st as not thine
          own: 355
Thou art their author and prime architect;
For I no sooner in my heart divined
(My heart, which by a secret harmony
Still moves with thine, joined in connexion sweet)
That thou on Earth hadst prospered, which thy
          looks   360
Now also evidence, but straight I felt,
Though distant from thee worlds between, yet felt
That I must after thee with this thy son;
Such fatal consequence unites us three.

Hell could no longer hold us in her bounds,   365
Nor this unvoyageable gulf obscure
Detain from following thy illustrious track.
Thou hast achieved our liberty, confined
Within Hell-gates till now; thou us empowered
To fortify thus far and overlay   370
With this portentous bridge the dark abyss.
Thine now is all this world; thy virtue hath won
What thy hands builded not, thy wisdom gained
With odds what war hath lost and fully avenged
Our foil in Heaven: here thou shalt monarch
    reign,   375
There didst not; there let him still victor sway,
As battle hath adjudged, from this new world
Retiring, by his own doom alienated,
And henceforth monarchy with thee divide
Of all things, parted by the empyreal bounds,   380
His quadrature, from thy orbicular world,
Or try thee now more dangerous to his throne."
    Whom thus the Prince of Darkness answered glad:
"Fair daughter and thou son and grandchild both,
High proof ye now have given to be the race   385
Of Satan (for I glory in the name,
Antagonist of Heaven's almighty king),
Amply have merited of me, of all
The infernal empire, that so near Heaven's door
Triumphal with triumphal act have met,   390
Mine with this glorious work, and made one realm
Hell and this world—one realm, one continent
Of easy thoroughfare. Therefore, while I
Descend through darkness on your road with ease
To my associate powers, them to acquaint   395

With these successes and with them rejoice,
You two this way, among these numerous orbs,
All yours, right down to Paradise descend;
There dwell and reign in bliss; thence on the Earth
Dominion exercise and in the air,   400
Chiefly on man, sole lord of all declared;
Him first make sure your thrall and lastly kill.
My substitutes I send ye and create
Plenipotent on Earth, of matchless might
Issuing from me: on your joint vigour now   405
My hold of this new kingdom all depends,
Through Sin to Death exposed by my exploit.
If your joint power prevail, the affairs of Hell
No detriment need fear; go and be strong."

   So saying, he dismissed them; they with speed 410
Their course through thickest constellations held,
Spreading their bane; the blasted stars looked wan,
And planets, planet-struck, real eclipse
Then suffered. The other way Satan went down
The causey to Hell-gate; on either side   415
Disparted Chaos over-built exclaimed
And with rebounding surge the bars assailed,
That scorned his indignation. Through the gate,
Wide open and unguarded, Satan passed,
And all about found desolate; for those   420
Appointed to sit there had left their charge,
Flown to the upper world; the rest were all
Far to the inland retired, about the walls
Of Pandemonium, city and proud seat
Of Lucifer, so by allusion called   425
Of that bright star to Satan paragoned.
There kept their watch the legions, while the grand

In council sat, solicitous what chance
Might intercept their emperor sent; so he
Departing gave command, and they observed.   430
As when the Tartar from his Russian foe
By Astracan over the snowy plains
Retires, or Bactrian Sophi, from the horns
Of Turkish crescent, leaves all waste beyond
The realm of Aladule in his retreat   435
To Tauris or Casbeen: so these, the late
Heaven-banished host, left desert utmost Hell
Many a dark league, reduced in careful watch
Round their metropolis and now expecting
Each hour their great adventurer from the search   440
Of foreign worlds. He through the midst unmarked,
In show plebeian angel militant
Of lowest order, passed; and, from the door
Of that Plutonian hall, invisible
Ascended his high throne, which, under state   445
Of richest texture spread, at the upper end
Was placed in regal lustre. Down a while
He sat and round about him saw unseen.
At last, as from a cloud, his fulgent head
And shape star-bright appeared, or brighter clad   450
With what permissive glory since his fall
Was left him or false glitter. All amazed
At that so sudden blaze, the Stygian throng
Bent their aspect and whom they wished beheld,
Their mighty chief returned: loud was the acclaim. 455
Forth rushed in haste the great consulting peers,
Raised from their dark divan, and with like joy
Congratulant approached him, who with hand
Silence, and with these words attention won:

"Thrones, Dominations, Princedoms, Virtues,
    Powers— 460
For in possession such not only of right
I call ye and declare ye now, returned,
Successful beyond hope, to lead ye forth
Triumphant out of this infernal pit
Abominable, accursed, the house of woe, 465
And dungeon of our tyrant. Now possess,
As lords, a spacious world, to our native Heaven
Little inferior, by my adventure hard
With peril great achieved. Long were to tell
What I have done, what suffered, with what pain 470
Voyaged the unreal, vast, unbounded deep
Of horrible confusion, over which
By Sin and Death a broad way now is paved
To expedite your glorious march; but I
Toiled out my uncouth passage, forced to ride 475
The untractable abyss, plunged in the womb
Of unoriginal Night and Chaos wild,
That, jealous of their secrets, fiercely opposed
My journey strange, with clamorous uproar
Protesting fate supreme; thence how I found 480
The new-created world, which fame in Heaven
Long had foretold, a fabric wonderful,
Of absolute perfection; therein man
Placed in a Paradise, by our exile
Made happy. Him by fraud I have seduced 485
From his creator, and, the more to increase
Your wonder, with an apple! He, thereat
Offended—worth your laughter!—hath given up
Both his beloved man and all this world
To Sin and Death a prey, and so to us 490

Without our hazard, labour, or alarm,
To range in and to dwell and over man
To rule, as over all he should have ruled.
True is, me also he hath judged, or rather
Me not, but the brute serpent, in whose shape   495
Man I deceived: that which to me belongs
Is enmity, which he will put between
Me and mankind; I am to bruise his heel;
His seed (when is not set) shall bruise my head:
A world who would not purchase with a bruise   500
Or much more grievous pain? Ye have the account
Of my performance; what remains, ye gods,
But up and enter now into full bliss?"
    So having said, a while he stood, expecting
Their universal shout and high applause   505
To fill his ear; when, contrary, he hears
On all sides from innumerable tongues
A dismal universal hiss, the sound
Of public scorn. He wondered but not long
Had leisure, wondering at himself now more: 510
His visage drawn he felt to sharp and spare,
His arms clung to his ribs, his legs entwining
Each other, till, supplanted, down he fell
A monstrous serpent on his belly prone,
Reluctant, but in vain; a greater power   515
Now ruled him, punished in the shape he sinned,
According to his doom. He would have spoke,
But hiss for hiss returned with forked tongue
To forked tongue; for now were all transformed
Alike, to serpents all, as accessories   520
To his bold riot. Dreadful was the din
Of hissing through the hall, thick-swarming now

With complicated monsters, head and tail,
Scorpion and asp and amphisbæna dire,
Cerastes horned, hydrus and ellops drear   525
And dipsas (not so thick swarmed once the soil
Bedropt with blood of Gorgon, or the isle
Ophiusa): but still greatest he the midst,
Now dragon grown, larger than whom the sun
Engendered in the Pythian vale on slime,   530
Huge Python; and his power no less he seemed
Above the rest still to retain. They all
Him followed, issuing forth to the open field,
Where all yet left of that revolted rout,
Heaven-fallen, in station stood or just array,   535
Sublime with expectation when to see
In triumph issuing forth their glorious chief.
They saw, but other sight instead, a crowd
Of ugly serpents. Horror on them fell
And horrid sympathy; for what they saw   540
They felt themselves now changing: down their arms,
Down fell both spear and shield; down they as fast
And the dire hiss renewed and the dire form
Catched by contagion, like in punishment
As in their crime. Thus was the applause they
          meant   545
Turned to exploding hiss, triumph to shame
Cast on themselves from their own mouths. There
          stood
A grove hard by, sprung up with this their change,
(His will who reigns above) to aggravate
Their penance, laden with fair fruit like that   550
Which grew in Paradise, the bait of Eve
Used by the tempter. On that prospect strange

Their earnest eyes they fixed, imagining
For one forbidden tree a multitude
Now risen to work them further woe or shame;   555
Yet, parched with scalding thirst and hunger fierce,
Though to delude them sent, could not abstain,
But on they rolled in heaps, and, up the trees
Climbing, sat thicker than the snaky locks
That curled Megæra. Greedily they plucked   560
The fruitage fair to sight, like that which grew
Near that bituminous lake where Sodom flamed;
This, more delusive, not the touch, but taste
Deceived: they, fondly thinking to allay
Their appetite with gust, instead of fruit   565
Chewed bitter ashes, which the offended taste
With spattering noise rejected. Oft they assayed,
Hunger and thirst constraining; drugged as oft,
With hatefulest disrelish writhed their jaws,
With soot and cinders filled; so oft they fell   570
Into the same illusion, not as man
Whom they triumphed once lapsed. Thus were they
     plagued
And worn with famine long and ceaseless hiss,
Till their lost shape, permitted, they resumed;
Yearly enjoined, some say, to undergo   575
This annual humbling certain numbered days,
To dash their pride and joy for man seduced.
However, some tradition they dispersed
Among the heathen of their purchase got
And fabled how the serpent, whom they called   580
Ophion, with Eurynome (the wide-
Encroaching Eve perhaps), had first the rule
Of high Olympus, thence by Saturn driven

And Ops, ere yet Dictæan Jove was born.

Meanwhile in Paradise the hellish pair 585
Too soon arrived; Sin there in power before,
Once actual, now in body and to dwell
Habitual habitant; behind her Death,
Close following pace for pace, not mounted yet
On his pale horse; to whom Sin thus began: 590

"Second of Satan sprung, all-conquering Death,
What think'st thou of our empire now, though
    earned
With travail difficult? not better far
Than still at Hell's dark threshold to have sat watch,
Unnamed, undreaded, and thyself half-starved?" 595

Whom thus the Sin-born monster answered soon:
"To me, who with eternal famine pine,
Alike is Hell or Paradise or Heaven:
There best, where most with ravin I may meet;
Which here, though plenteous, all too little seems 600
To stuff this maw, this vast unhide-bound corpse."

To whom the incestuous mother thus replied:
"Thou therefore on these herbs and fruits and flowers
Feed first; on each beast next and fish and fowl,
No homely morsels; and whatever thing 605
The scythe of time mows down devour unspared;
Till I, in man residing, through the race,
His thoughts, his looks, words, actions, all infect
And season him thy last and sweetest prey."

This said, they both betook them several ways, 610
Both to destroy or unimmortal make
All kinds and for destruction to mature
Sooner or later; which the Almighty seeing,
From his transcendent seat the saints among,

To those bright Orders uttered thus his voice: 615
  "See with what heat these dogs of Hell advance
To waste and havoc yonder world, which I
So fair and good created and had still
Kept in that state, had not the folly of man
Let in these wasteful furies, who impute   620
Folly to me (so doth the Prince of Hell
And his adherents), that with so much ease
I suffer them to enter and possess
A place so heavenly, and conniving seem
To gratify my scornful enemies,   625
That laugh, as if, transported with some fit
Of passion, I to them had quitted all,
At random yielded up to their misrule;
And know not that I called and drew them thither,
My Hell-hounds, to lick up the draff and filth   630
Which man's polluting sin with taint hath shed
On what was pure; till, crammed and gorged, nigh
    burst
With sucked and glutted offal, at one sling
Of thy victorious arm, well-pleasing Son,
Both Sin and Death and yawning grave at last,   635
Through Chaos hurled, obstruct the mouth of Hell
For ever and seal up his ravenous jaws.
Then Heaven and Earth, renewed, shall be made pure
To sanctity that shall receive no stain:
Till then the curse pronounced on both precedes."   640
  He ended, and the heavenly audience loud
Sung halleluiah, as the sound of seas
Through multitude that sung: "Just are thy ways,
Righteous are thy decrees on all thy works;
Who can extenuate thee?" Next, to the Son,   645

Destined restorer of mankind, by whom
New Heaven and Earth shall to the ages rise,
Or down from Heaven descend. Such was their song,
While the Creator, calling forth by name
His mighty angels, gave them several charge,   650
As sorted best with present things. The sun
Had first his precept so to move, so shine,
As might affect the Earth with cold and heat
Scarce tolerable and from the north to call
Decrepit winter, from the south to bring   655
Solstitial summer's heat. To the blanc moon
Her office they prescribed; to the other five
Their planetary motions and aspects,
In sextile, square and trine and opposite.
Of noxious efficacy, and when to join   660
In synod unbenign; and taught the fixed
Their influence malignant when to shower,
Which of them rising with the sun or falling
Should prove tempestuous. To the winds they set
Their corners, when with bluster to confound   665
Sea, air, and shore; the thunder when to roll
With terror through the dark aerial hall.
Some say he bid his angels turn askance
The poles of Earth twice ten degrees and more
From the sun's axle; they with labour pushed   670
Oblique the centric globe: some say the sun
Was bid turn reins from the equinoctial road
Like distant breadth to Taurus with the seven
Atlantic Sisters and the Spartan Twins
Up to the Tropic Crab thence down amain   675
By Leo and the Virgin and the Scales
As deep as Capricorn, to bring in change

Of seasons to each clime: else had the spring
Perpetual smiled on Earth with vernant flowers,
Equal in days and nights, except to those   680
Beyond the polar circles; to them day
Had unbenighted shone, while the low sun,
To recompense his distance, in their sight
Had rounded still the horizon and not known
Or east or west; which had forbid the snow   685
From cold Estotiland and south as far
Beneath Magellan. At that tasted fruit
The sun as from Thyestean banquet turned
His course intended: else how had the world
Inhabited, though sinless, more than now   690
Avoided pinching cold and scorching heat?
These changes in the heavens, though slow, produced
Like change on sea and land: sideral blast,
Vapour and mist and exhalation hot,
Corrupt and pestilent. Now from the north   695
Of Norumbega and the Samoed shore,
Bursting their brazen dungeon, armed with ice
And snow and hail and stormy gust and flaw,
Boreas and Cæcias and Argestes loud
And Thracias rend the woods and seas upturn;   700
With adverse blasts upturns them from the south
Notus and Afer black with thundrous clouds
From Serraliona; thwart of these as fierce
Forth rush the Levant and the Ponent winds,
Eurus and Zephyr with their lateral noise,   705
Sirocco and Libecchio. Thus began
Outrage from lifeless things; but Discord first,
Daughter of Sin, among the irrational
Death introduced through fierce antipathy:

Beast now with beast 'gan war and fowl with fowl   710
And fish with fish; to graze the herb all leaving
Devoured each other; nor stood much in awe
Of man, but fled him or with countenance grim
Glared on him passing. These were from without
The growing miseries which Adam saw   715
Already in part, though hid in gloomiest shade,
To sorrow abandoned; but worse felt within
And, in a troubled sea of passion tost,
Thus to disburden sought with sad complaint:
   "O miserable of happy! is this the end   720
Of this new glorious world and me so late
The glory of that glory, who now, become
Accursed of blessed, hide me from the face
Of God, whom to behold was then my highth
Of happiness? Yet well, if here would end   725
The misery; I deserved it and would bear
My own deservings; but this will not serve:
All that I eat or drink or shall beget
Is propagated curse. O voice, once heard
Delightfully, 'Increase and multiply';   730
Now death to hear! for what can I increase
Or multiply but curses on my head?
Who, of all ages to succeed, but, feeling
The evil on him brought by me, will curse
My head? 'Ill fare our ancestor impure!   735
For this we may thank Adam!' but his thanks
Shall be the execration; so, besides
Mine own that bide upon me, all from me
Shall with a fierce reflux on me redound,
On me, as on their natural centre, light   740
Heavy, though in their place. O fleeting joys

Of Paradise, dear bought with lasting woes!
Did I request thee, Maker, from my clay
To mould me man? did I solicit thee
From darkness to promote me or here place   745
In this delicious garden? As my will
Concurred not to my being, it were but right
And equal to reduce me to my dust,
Desirous to resign and render back
All I received, unable to perform   750
Thy terms too hard, by which I was to hold
The good I sought not. To the loss of that,
Sufficient penalty, why hast thou added
The sense of endless woes? Inexplicable
Thy justice seems. Yet, to say truth, too late   755
I thus contest; then should have been refused
Those terms whatever, when they were proposed.
Thou didst accept them: wilt thou enjoy the good,
Then cavil the conditions? And though God
Made thee without thy leave, what if thy son   760
Prove disobedient, and, reproved, retort,
'Wherefore didst thou beget me? I sought it not.'
Wouldst thou admit for his contempt of thee
That proud excuse? yet him not thy election
But natural necessity begot.   765
God made thee of choice his own, and of his own
To serve him; thy reward was of his grace;
Thy punishment then justly is at his will.
Be it so, for I submit; his doom is fair,
That dust I am and shall to dust return.   770
O welcome hour whenever! Why delays
His hand to execute what his decree
Fixed on this day? why do I overlive?

Why am I mocked with death and lengthened out
To deathless pain? How gladly would I meet   775
Mortality, my sentence, and be earth
Insensible, how glad would lay me down
As in my mother's lap! There I should rest
And sleep secure; his dreadful voice no more
Would thunder in my ears; no fear of worse   780
To me and to my offspring would torment me
With cruel expectation. Yet one doubt
Pursues me still, lest all I cannot die;
Lest that pure breath of life, the spirit of man
Which God inspired, cannot together perish   785
With this corporeal clod; then, in the grave
Or in some other dismal place, who knows
But I shall die a living death? O thought
Horrid, if true! Yet why? It was but breath
Of life that sinned: what dies but what had life   790
And sin? the body properly hath neither.
All of me then shall die: let this appease
The doubt, since human reach no further knows.
For though the Lord of all be infinite,
Is his wrath also? Be it, man is not so,   795
But mortal doomed. How can he exercise
Wrath without end on man, whom death must end?
Can he make deathless death? That were to make
Strange contradiction; which to God himself,
Impossible is held, as argument   800
Of weakness not of power. Will he draw out
For anger's sake finite to infinite
In punished man, to satify his rigour
Satisfied never? That were to extend
His sentence beyond dust and nature's law;   805

By which all causes else according still
To the reception of their matter act,
Not to the extent of their own sphere. But say
That death be not one stroke, as I supposed,
Bereaving sense, but endless misery   810
From this day onward, which I feel begun
Both in me and without me, and so last
To perpetuity: ay me! that fear
Comes thundering back with dreadful revolution
On my defenceless head. Both Death and I   815
Am found eternal and incorporate both:
Nor I on my part single; in me all
Posterity stands cursed. Fair patrimony
That I must leave ye, sons! Oh, were I able
To waste it all myself and leave ye none!   820
So disinherited, how would ye bless
Me, now your curse! Ah, why should all mankind
For one man's fault thus guiltless be condemned,
If guiltless? But from me what can proceed
But all corrupt, both mind and will depraved   825
Not to do only but to will the same
With me? How can they then acquitted stand
In sight of God? Him, after all disputes,
Forced I absolve; all my evasions vain
And reasonings, though through mazes, lead me
          still   830
But to my own conviction: first and last
On me, me only, as the source and spring
Of all corruption, all the blame lights due.
So might the wrath! Fond wish! Couldst thou
          support
That burden, heavier than the Earth to bear,   835

Than all the World much heavier, though divided
With that bad woman? Thus, what thou desir'st
And what thou fear'st alike destroys all hope
Of refuge and concludes thee miserable
Beyond all past example and future;   840
To Satan only like, both crime and doom.
O conscience, into what abyss of fears
And horrors hast thou driven me; out of which
I find no way, from deep to deeper plunged!"

    Thus Adam to himself lamented loud   845
Through the still night, not now, as ere man fell,
Wholesome and cool and mild but with black air
Accompanied, with damps and dreadful gloom;
Which to his evil conscience represented
All things with double terror. On the ground   850
Outstretched he lay, on the cold ground, and oft
Cursed his creation; Death as oft accused
Of tardy execution, since denounced
The day of his offence. "Why comes not Death,"
Said he, "with one thrice-acceptable stroke   855
To end me? Shall Truth fail to keep her word,
Justice divine not hasten to be just?
But Death comes not at call; Justice divine
Mends not her slowest pace for prayers or cries.
O woods, O fountains, hillocks, dales, and
    bowers,   860
With other echo late I taught your shades
To answer and resound far other song."
Whom thus afflicted when sad Eve beheld,
Desolate where she sat, approaching nigh,
Soft words to his fierce passion she assayed;   865
But her with stern regard he thus repelled:

"Out of my sight, thou serpent! that name best
Befits thee, with him leagued, thyself as false
And hateful: nothing wants, but that thy shape
Like his and colour serpentine may show   870
Thy inward fraud, to warn all creatures from thee
Henceforth; lest that too heavenly form, pretended
To hellish falsehood, snare them. But for thee
I had persisted happy, had not thy pride
And wandering vanity, when least was safe,   875
Rejected my forewarning and disdained
Not to be trusted, longing to be seen,
Though by the Devil himself, him overweening
To overreach; but, with the serpent meeting,
Fooled and beguiled; by him thou, I by thee,   880
To trust thee from my side, imagined wise,
Constant, mature, proof against all assaults;
And understood not all was but a show
Rather than solid virtue, all but a rib
Crooked by nature (bent, as now appears,   885
More to the part sinister) from me drawn;
Well if thrown out, as supernumerary
To my just number found! Oh, why did God,
Creator wise, that peopled highest Heaven
With spirits masculine, create at last   890
This novelty on Earth, this fair defect
Of nature and not fill the world at once
With men, as angels, without feminine;
Or find some other way to generate
Mankind? This mischief had not then befallen,   895
And more that shall befall: innumerable
Disturbances on Earth through female snares
And strait conjunction with this sex. For either

He never shall find out fit mate but such
As some misfortune brings him or mistake;　　900
Or whom he wishes most shall seldom gain,
Through her perverseness, but shall see her gained
By a far worse, or, if she love, withheld
By parents; or his happiest choice too late
Shall meet, already linked and wedlock-bound　　905
To a fell adversary, his hate or shame:
Which infinite calamity shall cause
To human life and household peace confound."
　　He added not and from her turned; but Eve,
Not so repulsed, with tears that ceased not flowing　910
And tresses all disordered, at his feet
Fell humble and, embracing them, besought
His peace and thus proceeded in her plaint:
　　"Forsake me not thus, Adam; witness Heaven
What love sincere and reverence in my heart　　915
I bear thee and unweeting have offended,
Unhappily deceived! Thy suppliant
I beg and clasp thy knees; bereave me not,
Whereon I live, thy gentle looks, thy aid,
Thy counsel in this uttermost distress,　　920
My only strength and stay: forlorn of thee,
Whither shall I betake me, where subsist?
While yet we live, scarce one short hour perhaps,
Between us two let there be peace; both joining,
As joined in injuries, one enmity　　925
Against a foe by doom express assigned us,
That cruel serpent. On me exercise not
Thy hatred for this misery befallen;
On me already lost, me than thyself
More miserable. Both have sinned; but thou　　930

Against God only; I against God and thee,
And to the place of judgment will return,
There with my cries importune Heaven that all
The sentence, from thy head removed, may light
On me, sole cause to thee of all this woe,   935
Me, me only, just object of his ire."
    She ended weeping; and her lowly plight,
Immovable till peace obtained from fault
Acknowledged and deplored, in Adam wrought
Commiseration. Soon his heart relented   940
Towards her, his life so late and sole delight,
Now at his feet submissive in distress,
Creature so fair his reconcilement seeking,
His counsel, whom she had displeased, his aid.
As one disarmed, his anger all he lost   945
And thus with peaceful words upraised her soon:
    "Unwary, and too desirous, as before
So now, of what thou know'st not, who desir'st
The punishment all on thyself! Alas,
Bear thine own first, ill able to sustain   950
His full wrath, whose thou feel'st as yet least part,
And my displeasure bear'st so ill. If prayers
Could alter high decrees, I to that place
Would speed before thee and be louder heard,
That on my head all might be visited,   955
Thy frailty and infirmer sex forgiven,
To me committed and by me exposed.
But rise; let us no more contend nor blame
Each other, blamed enough elsewhere, but strive
In offices of love, how we may lighten   960
Each other's burden in our share of woe;
Since this day's death denounced, if aught I see,

Will prove no sudden but a slow-paced evil,
A long day's dying to augment our pain,
And to our seed (O hapless seed!) derived."   965
    To whom thus Eve, recovering heart, replied:
"Adam, by sad experiment I know
How little weight my words with thee can find,
Found so erroneous, thence by just event
Found so unfortunate; nevertheless,   970
Restored by thee, vile as I am, to place
Of new acceptance, hopeful to regain
Thy love, the sole contentment of my heart,
Living or dying from thee I will not hide
What thoughts in my unquiet breast are risen,   975
Tending to some relief of our extremes,
Or end, though sharp and sad, yet tolerable
As in our evils and of easier choice.
If care of our descent perplex us most,
Which must be born to certain woe, devoured   980
By Death at last (and miserable it is
To be to others cause of misery,
Our own begotten, and of our loins to bring
Into this cursed world a woeful race,
That after wretched life must be at last   985
Food for so foul a monster), in thy power
It lies, yet ere conception, to prevent
The race unblest, to being yet unbegot.
Childless thou art, childless remain; so Death
Shall be deceived his glut and with us two   990
Be forced to satisfy his ravenous maw.
But if thou judge it hard and difficult,
Conversing, looking, loving, to abstain
From love's due rites, nuptial embraces sweet,

And with desire to languish without hope 995
Before the present object languishing
With like desire, which would be misery
And torment less than none of what we dread;
Then, both our selves and seed at once to free
From what we fear for both, let us make short, 1000
Let us seek Death, or, he not found, supply
With our own hands his office on ourselves.
Why stand we longer shivering under fears
That show no end but death, and have the power,
Of many ways to die the shortest choosing, 1005
Destruction with destruction to destroy?"

   She ended here, or vehement despair
Broke off the rest; so much of death her thoughts
Had entertained as dyed her cheeks with pale.
But Adam, with such counsel nothing swayed, 1010
To better hopes his more attentive mind
Labouring had raised and thus to Eve replied:
   "Eve, thy contempt of life and pleasure seems
To argue in thee something more sublime
And excellent than what thy mind contemns; 1015
But self-destruction therefore sought refutes
That excellence thought in thee and implies,
Not thy contempt, but anguish and regret
For loss of life and pleasure overloved.
Or if thou covet death, as utmost end 1020
Of misery, so thinking to evade
The penalty pronounced, doubt not but God
Hath wiselier armed his vengeful ire than so
To be forestalled; much more I fear lest death
So snatched will not exempt us from the pain 1025
We are by doom to pay; rather such acts

Of contumacy will provoke the Highest
To make death in us live. Then let us seek
Some safer resolution, which methinks
I have in view, calling to mind with heed   1030
Part of our sentence, that thy seed shall bruise
The serpent's head: piteous amends, unless
Be meant, whom I conjecture, our grand foe,
Satan, who in the serpent hath contrived
Against us this deceit. To crush his head   1035
Would be revenge indeed; which will be lost
By death brought on ourselves or childless days
Resolved as thou proposest; so our foe
Shall scape his punishment ordained, and we
Instead shall double ours upon our heads.   1040
No more be mentioned then of violence
Against ourselves and wilful barrenness,
That cuts us off from hope and savours only
Rancour and pride, impatience and despite,
Reluctance against God and his just yoke   1045
Laid on our necks. Remember with what mild
And gracious temper he both heard and judged,
Without wrath or reviling; we expected
Immediate dissolution, which we thought
Was meant by death that day; when, lo! to thee   1050
Pains only in child-bearing were foretold,
And bringing forth, soon recompensed with joy,
Fruit of thy womb. On me the curse aslope
Glanced on the ground: with labour I must earn
My bread. What harm? idleness had been worse;   1055
My labour will sustain me; and, lest cold
Or heat should injure us, his timely care
Hath, unbesought, provided, and his hands

Clothed us unworthy, pitying while he judged.
How much more, if we pray him, will his ear   1060
Be open, and his heart to pity incline
And teach us further by what means to shun
The inclement seasons, rain, ice, hail, and snow,
Which now the sky with various face begins
To show us in this mountain, while the winds   1065
Blow moist and keen, shattering the graceful locks
Of these fair spreading trees; which bids us seek
Some better shroud, some better warmth to cherish
Our limbs benumbed, ere this diurnal star
Leave cold the night, how we his gathered beams   1070
Reflected may with matter sere foment
Or by collision of two bodies grind
The air attrite to fire; as late the clouds,
Justling or pushed with winds, rude in their shock,
Tine the slant lightning, whose thwart flame driven
        down   1075
Kindles the gummy bark of fir or pine
And sends a comfortable heat from far,
Which might supply the sun. Such fire to use,
And what may else be remedy or cure
To evils which our own misdeeds have wrought,   1080
He will instruct us praying and of grace
Beseeching him; so as we need not fear
To pass commodiously this life, sustained
By him with many comforts, till we end
In dust, our final rest and native home.   1085
What better can we do, than, to the place
Repairing where he judged us, prostrate fall
Before him reverent and there confess
Humbly our faults and pardon beg, with tears

Watering the ground and with our sighs the air 1090
Frequenting, sent from hearts contrite in sign
Of sorrow unfeigned and humiliation meek?
Undoubtedly he will relent and turn
From his displeasure; in whose look serene,
When angry most he seemed and most severe, 1095
What else but favour, grace, and mercy shone?"

    So spake our father penitent; nor Eve
Felt less remorse. They, forthwith to the place
Repairing where he judged them, prostrate fell
Before him reverent and both confessed 1100
Humbly their faults and pardon begged, with tears
Watering the ground and with their sighs the air
Frequenting, sent from hearts contrite, in sign
Of sorrow unfeigned and humiliation meek.

NOTES

Book IX

THIS books opens abruptly even stormily; and the opening is meant to contrast with the quiet ending of Book Eight, where Raphael, the genial archangel, takes his leave after much familiar talk with Adam and Eve. There will now be no more of such talk; and what follows will be either tragic action or talk with a reproving God or with the military archangel, Michael. Here, for the fourth time, Milton speaks at length in his own person; and these personal passages mark the different main stages of the poem and are thus an organic part of it.

1-4. *angel guest* refers to the Archangel Raphael, whose visit to Adam and Eve in Paradise has occupied the four previous books. And the visit included a meal. Most commentators have taken *god* to refer to the visit of God the Father to Paradise to create Eve. But this is impossible, for God neither *sat indulgent* nor *partook rural repast*. When Milton says *god* he is thinking not only of his own poetry but of the stories, sacred and pagan, of the gods visiting men in disguise and eating with them. One such is in *Genesis* xviii, where three representatives of God, disguised as men, appear to Abraham and are entertained by him; and another is the tale of Philemon and Baucis, told by Ovid in *Metamorphoses*, viii, 611-724. These entertained Jupiter and Mercury, disguised as men. In short Milton says, "I have finished with the type of literature in which the gods pay genial visits to men and eat with them (to which type my account of Raphael visiting Adam and Eve belongs)."

5. *Venial* here means not as usually *pardonable* but *permissible*.

6. *tragic* is probably an adjective agreeing with *notes* understood; but it could mean *the tragic*, being a noun. *foul distrust etc*. To satisfy grammar one can make these words governed by *change to*, understood, but Milton was fond of vague appositions where the reader must mentally supply the appropriate connection. Here the reader must supply something like "I will recount."

8. *disobedience*. The word must have been more powerful in Milton's day than in ours: it comes here as a climax and it is the key word of the whole poem, which begins, "Of man's first disobedience."

9. *distance and distaste*: a deliberate jangle to denote discord.

11. The line recalls the third line of the poem, "Brought death into the world, and all our woe." Milton recalls the reader to the violent and tragic tone of the poem's beginning.

12. *shadow*, 'follower'. *Misery*, 'pain and sickness.'

13. *harbinger*, 'forerunner.' *argument*, 'subject.'

14–19. Milton claims that the subject of the loss of Paradise is nobler than those of the great heroic poems of antiquity: of the *Iliad*, where Achilles chased Hector three times round the walls of Troy; of the *Odyssey*, whose hero Odysseus incurred the anger of Neptune; of Virgil's *Aeneid*, which recounts how Turnus had to yield his betrothed, Lavinia, to Aeneas and how Aeneas was the victim of Juno's hate.

20. *answerable style*, 'style to correspond to the nobility of the subject chosen.'

21. *celestial patroness*, 'Urania.' Milton invoked her at the beginning of the poem. She was properly the Muse of

astronomy, but he extends her province to that of heavenly or sacred poetry.

22–24. A piece of autobiography. Like other poets Milton testifies to the experience of poetry coming to the poet of itself without any apparent effort of the will. A. E. Housman records how "there would flow into my mind, with sudden and unaccountable emotion, sometimes a line or two of verse, sometimes a whole stanza at once." But Milton's habit of composing at night was peculiar. An early biography, anonymous but by one of his friends, states that Milton, "waking early, had commonly a good stock of verses ready against his amanuensis came; which if it happened to be later than ordinary, he would complain, saying *he wanted to be milked.*"

26. Milton first intended an epic on Arthur. Discarding this intention, he considered several subjects including one on Alfred. Settling finally on the loss of Paradise he was delayed by the Civil War, his duties as a government official, and by his blindness. It was not till he was about forty-eight that he began finally on the composition of his poem.

29. *chief maistry*, a typically Miltonic apposition, meaning "the special skill or mastery of such poems being . . ."

29–31. *dissect* is scornfully used in its physical not its metaphorical sense. Milton means us to think of the anatomist's dissecting table and the butcher's yard and he satirises both the minute physical details of wounds found in the *Iliad* and *Aeneid* and the exaggerated *melées* of the medieval romances and of their progeny in the Italians, Boiardo and Ariosto. It was common for one of the principal knights in the medieval romances to kill a thousand men in a single battle.

33–38. Milton continues to refer to both classical and medieval heroic traditions, the games belonging to the first and the tournaments to the second.

34. *tilting furniture*, 'equipment for tournaments.' *emblazon'd*, 'inscribed with coats of arms.'

35. *Impreses*, 'emblematic devices.' *quaint* bears not its modern meaning but *elegant* or *ingenious*. *caparisons*, 'rich cloths spread over the horses' backs.'

36. *Bases* could refer either to the long skirts of the horses' trappings or to the knights' short skirts reaching from waist to knee. The first is more likely in the context. *tinsel* is a woven material with gold or silver thread interwoven and it connotes richness not, as to-day, tawdriness. *tinsel trappings* comes straight from Spenser, *Faerie Queene*. Milton included this poem and Sidney's *Arcadia* in the tradition he refers to.

37–38. The marshall arranged the seating; the sewer walked in before the courses and had them set on the tables; the seneschal was the household steward.

39. Yet another vague apposition. The meaning is that all these things are within the reach of mechanical skill and inferior capacity.

41. Milton writes *of* to go with *studious* though it should be *in* to go with *skill'd*, in the next line.

44–45. Many people in the seventeenth century thought that the world was in its old age. Milton, who admired the Italians, thought that their superior intelligence was due to their more southerly latitude. In his *History of Britain* he wrote, "For the sun, which we want, ripens wits as well as fruits; and as wine and oil are imported to us from abroad, so must ripe understanding and many civil virtues be imported." *wing*, 'flight.'

48. The narrative, now resumed, refers first to the end of Book Eight when evening approaches and Raphael sets out from Eden to Heaven, and then to the end of Book Four, where at dawn Gabriel and his angelic watch expel Satan from Paradise.

49. *Hesperus*, the evening star, Venus.

54–55. *now improved/In mediated fraud*: through what he had gathered in his journeys round the globe, about to be described.

56. *maugre*, 'in spite of.'

60–63. See IV, 125 and 555, where Uriel spied Satan and descended from the sun to warn Gabriel and his guard. Satan's anguish was due to his humiliation at having to fly before Gabriel, who, his inferior when both were in Heaven, now derives strength from God that reverses the position. In very human fashion Satan tries to conquer his anguish by speed.

64–66. Satan circled the earth, always keeping in darkness, seven times; thrice round the equator or *equinoctial line* and four times along the imaginary lines running north to south, the *colures*.

70. *Now not*, 'existing no more.'

71. *Paradise* is the mountain plateau where Adam and Eve lived, while *Eden* (see 77 below) is the district in which Paradise is set.

77–82. Satan's first journey was northward from Asia Minor, where Eden was situated, to the Black Sea (Pontus), to the inland sea of Azof (Pool Maeotis), and by the river Obi to the North Pole. His later journey was east to west from the river Orontes in Syria over the Mediterranean and Atlantic to the Isthmus of Panama (Darien) and across the Pacific to India, reaching first the Ganges and then the Indus, to which Eden was comparatively close.

86. *Cf. Genesis*, iii, 1, "Now the serpent was more subtil than any beast of the field which the Lord God had made." Understand *to be* after *serpent*: during his flight in the dark, Satan had made his observations and concluded thus about serpents. Accustomed to the gloom of Hell he could use his eyes in the dark.

87–88. *irresolute/Of thoughts revolv'd*, 'which long failed to solve the questions that turned in his head.' *sentence*, 'decision.'

89. *imp*, 'child' or 'product.'

92. After *sleights* understand *there should be*.

95. *Doubt*, 'suspicion.'

99 ff. This speech recalls what Milton had conveyed about Satan: that he was not sheer evil but goodness corrupted. Satan describes the earth in lines of great beauty but like Coleridge in his *Dejection, an Ode* he "sees not feels how beautiful" it is. That Satan can speak thus makes his vengeful and destructive thoughts the more tragic.

100. *gods*, 'angels.'

103. *heavens*, 'stars.'

104. *officious*, 'serviceable' or 'useful.'

105. *as seems*. Verity thinks Milton here guards himself against the possibility that other stars, the moon for instance, may be inhabited. Milton had suggested (iii, 460–2) that beings "betwixt th' angelical and human kind" may inhabit the moon.

113. *all summ'd up in man*. According to the traditional scheme inherited from the Greeks man contained within himself the faculty of growth, which was the peculiar property of vegetables, the faculty of sensation, which was the peculiar property of the lower animals, while his own peculiar property of reason was added to these.

115. *sweet interchange*. This could be the vocative and refer back to *thee*; but more likely *thee* refers to the earth and *sweet interchange* is in vague apposition and requires the insertion before it of some such ideas as "how I could have enjoyed!"

118–119. Note how the mention of *cave* leads naturally to the idea of refuge and of Satan's need for it. *place*, 'resting place.'

121–122. *siege/Of contraries*, 'location, hence exhibition, of things contrary to his own state of mind.'

130. *him*, 'man.'

132-133. *all this will soon/Follow*, 'all this natural beauty will soon become corrupt like man.'

146-147. *if they at least/Are his created*. Satan here repeats the arch-blasphemy he uttered to the bad angels after their revolt: that they may be self-created and not the work of God after all. See v. 859-61: "We know no time when we were not as now;/Know none before us, self-begot, self-raised/By our own quickening power."

150. *original*, 'first matter.'

155-157. From the general thought that God allows angels to minister to man Satan abruptly turns to Gabriel and his guard, whom he both hates and fears, and to the action he now prepares.

157. Milton probably wanted *earthy* to mean both *earthly* and *low*. Satan continues to rub in the indignity of angels having to do with their inferior, man. In Milton's days the word could bear both meanings.

164. *constrained*: another instance of Milton making a word do more than one job of work. Satan says he is *compressed* into a beast and is *compelled* to invest with flesh and to brutalise his airy and rarefied angelic substance.

167. *highth*, height, (compare *depth*), the common Miltonic form.

170. *obnoxious*, 'liable.'

174. *higher*, 'of my higher aim,' *i.e.* God.

176 *son of despite*: usually taken as a Hebraism (like *son of valour* meaning valorous man) and itself meaning *contemptible creature*, but more pointed if meaning *result of God's envy*, the next line enlarging on this thought.

178. Robert Thyer (1709-1781) wrote truly of Satan's long speech: "There is all the horror and malignity of a fiendlike spirit expressed, and yet this is so artfully tempered with Satan's sudden starts of recollection upon the meanness and folly of what he was going to undertake,

as plainly show the remains of the archangel and the ruins of a superior nature."

186. *nocent*, 'poisonous.'

188. *brutal*, 'brutish.'

190. *act intelligential*, 'an activity of mind beyond the brutish.'

191. *close*, 'intently.'

200. *The season, prime for.* . . . There were as yet no seasons (in the usual sense of the word) in Paradise, the place enjoying perpetual spring. *Season* here means time of day, namely the dawn, which is best for scents and fresh breezes

201. *commune*, 'discuss together.'

205. *still*, 'incessantly.'

218. *spring*, 'thicket.'

229. *motion'd*, 'proposed.'

239. *reason* here means more than mere *reasoning power*; it is the highest human faculty and the one that distinguishes man from the beasts. Its two great divisions were the understanding and the will.

245. *wilderness*, 'wildness.'

250. *short retirement*, 'retirement even if short.'

265. *Or this*, 'whether his design be this.'

270. *virgin*, 'virginal, pure, innocent.'

272. *austere* excludes the possibility of a smile, and Milton probably wishes us to recall for a moment what Adam said a few lines back about smiles as the food of love.

276. Eve's innocent admission of eavesdropping marks the beginning of the comic strain that, though subordinate, runs through this book.

279. *my*, emphatic. Note the growing conversational cadence of Eve's speech.

284. 'We may be immune from his violence, or, if we are not, we can repel it.'

289. *misthought* has been explained as a noun, meaning mis

judgment, in apposition to *thoughts* in the line before. More likely it is the passive participle, meaning 'unjustly thought.'

292. *entire from*, 'untouched by.'

293. *Not diffident of thee*, 'it is not because I distrust you that . . .'

310. *Access*, 'increase.'

314. *and rais'd unite*, 'and, the utmost vigour having been raised, shame would go on to make all the virtues mentioned, wisdom watchfulness strength, work together.'

320. *attributed*. Accent on first syllable.

326. *still*. See 205.

330. *front*, 'forehead.'

334. *event*, 'outcome.'

335–336. *unassayed/Alone*, 'if not tested in solitude.'

338. *Left*, 'to have been left.'

339. Understand *us* before *single*.

342. Adam's speech expresses two doctrines about which Milton felt strongly: the freedom of the will to choose either good or evil and the need for humility. Man was created self-sufficient, he need not by the terms of his creation choose evil, but unless he has the option of so doing he is not a moral being at all. Milton asserts the doctrine of humility less obviously through Adam's telling Eve not to seek temptation. To seek this, as Eve had virtually implied you should do, is not courage but rashness, not good sense but pride. There is all the difference between asking for trouble and dealing courageously with trouble when it comes. But Milton also believed that a man should combine the utmost vigour of action with his humility. He makes Adam here say in all humility, "Seek not temptation then," but he said in his own *Areopagitica*, "I cannot praise a fugitive and cloistered virtue, unexercised and unbreathed, that never sallies out and seeks her adversary, but slinks out of the

race, where that immortal garland is to be run for, not without dust and heat.'' Eve's mistake was to advance the second doctrine, without qualifying it with the first. It is mere folly to sally out and seek an adversary until you know who he is and what are his resources.

352. *Reason* means here the <u>understanding</u> rather than man's higher capacities generally. Reason is *right* or works truly, provided it is not duped. And the function of reason is to supply the will with the correct data.

353. *ware*, 'wary.' *erect*, 'alert.'

358. mind, 'remind.'

361. *specious* and *suborned*. Milton may be glancing at the Latin derivation of these two words as well as using them in their common sense. *Speciosus* meant primarily *beautiful* and *ornare* meant *to adorn* before it meant to *equip*. Milton thus conveys the sense that the seducing object may have a touch of beauty.

367. *approve thy constancy*, 'give proof of your fortitude.'

368. *obedience*, of wife to husband. Milton was quite certain of the justice of the doctrine but not more so than his contemporaries. In the present context the tragedy is that Adam, having pronounced the doctrine, fails to enforce it, for immediately after he not only lets Eve have her way in a course he thought wrong but finds a far-fetched reason in favour of it. I even believe that Milton had the subtlety to imply that Eve, at the point where Adam yields to her, actually wanted him to assert himself.

70-371. *secure* bore the senses of *free from care* and *too little on one's guard* as well as the usual one. Verity paraphrased the lines thus: 'It may be that if we remain together and let the trial come to us, instead of going to meet it, we shall not be so well prepared for it when it does come as you appear to be after my warning.'

372. As Eve had misused the Miltonic doctrine of not praising a fugitive and cloistered virtue, so Adam here

abuses the Miltonic doctrine of freedom. Freedom for Milton consisted of freedom of choice within definite limits existing in nature or ordained by God. Adam failed to qualify Eve's freedom of choice by the woman's natural obligation to yield to the man's judgment in truly momentous issues. For the woman here not to yield and for the man not to exact obedience was to go against the order of things and was not freedom but disorder.

377. Even at this turning point there is an element of comedy. Eve gets it both ways: she appears submissive but has the last word; and she neatly shifts the responsibility on Adam by pretending that the main reason for persisting in her plan to garden alone is his feeble defence of such an act. She also (383) calls herself the weaker just after she has got her own way. Nevertheless she retains her charm throughout.

385–386. *hand/Soft*, 'hand softly' or 'soft hand'? Possibly both.

387. *Oread*, mountain nymph. *Dryad*, wood nymph. *Delia*, the goddess Artemis or Diana, who was born in the island of Delos.

392. *Guiltless of fire*. That an art which does not know the use of fire should be more innocent than one which does seems a strange notion. Nevertheless there are several strands of traditional thought in it. In Greek mythology Prometheus was guilty of theft when he gave fire to mortal men, and Zeus punished him for it. Then fire suggests sophistication, not all of it good: the tortuous lore of alchemy, over-elaborate cooking, the brewing of poisons. Adam and Eve were perfectly healthy on their vegetarian, uncooked diet. And generally *guiltless* here points to the state of innocence in which the human pair were still living.

393. *Pales*, a Roman goddess of flocks and herds. *Pomona*, as her name signifies, was the Roman goddess of fruit.

Ovid recounts in *Metamorphoses*, xiv how Vertumnus, another country god, wooed and won her.

395. *Ceres*, the Roman goddess of agriculture.

396. Bentley called this line "a monster of a phrase," and so it is by the standards of ordinary prose. But its sense is obvious at first reading, and it is a masterly piece of poetical compression.

402–403. *And all things . . . repast*, best taken closely with *amid the bower*, understanding *with* after *And*.

405. *Of* depends on the general sense of 'over-confident' rather than on any of the three adjectives in the preceding line.

406. Consciously or not I believe Milton was here recalling the lines Iago speaks about Othello when he knows he has corrupted his mind definitively, "Not poppy nor mandragora/Nor all the drowsy syrops of the world/Shall ever medicine thee to that sweet sleep/Which thou owedst yesterday."

409. *imminent*, 'threatening.'

413. *Mere*, 'entire.' In some traditions the tempter was represented as only half snake.

419. *Their tendance*, 'the object of their care.'

434. *traversed*, accent on second syllable.

436. *voluble*, 'with rolling motion.'

438. *imbordered*, 'planted so as to make borders.' *hand*, 'handiwork.'

439–441. Adonis, loved by Venus, was killed by a boar. Rescued from the underworld by her prayers Venus kept him in a garden of surpassing beauty. Milton referred to this piece of myth at the end of *Comus*. Odysseus, son of Laertes, visited Phaeacia, where Alcinous ruled. Alcinous had wonderful gardens with trees growing blossoms and fruit at the same time. See Homer *Odyssey*, vii, 112 ff.

442–443. *not mystic*, 'not imaginary.' This garden is real because referred to in Scripture. *sapient king*, Solomon who "made affinity with Pharaoh king of Egypt and took Pharoah's daughter and brought her into the city of David." (1 *Kings* iii, 1). The authority for the garden is *Song of Solomon*, vi.

445 ff. In Milton's day London was so small that it was easy to walk out of it into the country.

446. *houses thick*, a compressed phrase meaning the crowding together of the houses preventing the circulation of air. *annoy*, 'make foul.' This part of the simile corresponds to the darkness Satan had for days been living in and to his own foul and dangerous thoughts.

450. *tedded*. To *ted* is to scatter. Grass spread out to dry smells especially sweet.

453. *for her*, 'on her account.'

456. *plat*, 'plot.'

463. *That space*: not immediately clear, for no space of time has been mentioned. The probable meaning is 'while the spell of Eve's beauty and innocence was on him.'

465. *Stupidly* here has no touch of the modern sense of foolish but means 'in a state of stupour,' 'dazedly.'

471. *recollects*, probably 're-collects' or 'recovers' rather than in the modern sense of 'remembers.'

472. *gratulating*, 'gloating.'

475–476. nor hope/Of Paradise for Hell, 'nor has the hope of Paradise instead of Hell brought me here.'

477–478. *but all pleasure to destroy/Save what is in destroying*, 'but I have come here to destroy all pleasure except the very pleasure of destruction.'

481. *opportune*, 'conveniently placed.'

483. *intellectual*, 'intellect.'

485. *mould* does not mean 'shape' here but 'material.'

488. *to*, 'compared with.'

491. *not*, 'if not.'

493. *tend*, probably in the physical sense of 'pursue' and not in the abstract one of 'intend.'

497. *as since*, referring to God's punishment of the serpent for having beguiled Eve, "upon thy belly shalt thou go" (*Genesis*, iii, 14).

500. See *Hamlet* ii, 2, 457-458, "with eyes like carbuncles the hellish Pyrrhus/Old grandsire Priam seeks." The carbuncle was a red jewel.

502. *spires*, 'coils.'

503. *redundant*, 'billowing.'

504 ff. Ornamentation, such as the comparisons that follow, comes best in the pauses of the action. We now know for certain that Satan is to make his culminating attack on Eve and in that certainty we are glad to pause and enjoy the disgressive ornament that Milton gives us. The ornament serves also to emphasise what is to follow, hinting that it is too weighty and solemn to be entered on without ceremony. An example of similar technique is in Chaucer's *Knight's Tale*. We know at one point that the rival loves of Palamon and Arcite are to be settled by a tournament and because of that knowledge we welcome the elaborate account of the scenes depicted on the temples of Mars and Venus, where the two rivals go to offer their vows.

505-507. *Hermione and Cadmus*. Cadmus was king of Thebes and once prospered. Then he suffered many calamities, including the loss of all his descendants, till he and his wife, Harmonia or Hermione, were left solitary in old age. Going to Illyria, on the east coast of the Adriatic, they changed into serpents. Ovid told the story in *Metamorphoses*, iv, 562 ff., and Matthew Arnold made it the theme of one of his best lyrics, put into the mouth of Callicles in *Empedocles on Etna*, 427-460. *the god/In Epidaurus*. The relevant story is again from *Metamorphoses* (xv, 622-744). Aesculapius, son of Apollo, was god of healing. Advised by Apollo, Romans in time of plague sent to Epidaurus in Greece, the sanctuary of Aesculapius, for help. In the form of a snake the god allowed himself to be taken to Rome.

505. *changed*, intransitive.

507–510. *nor to which etc.*, 'nor were those serpents lovelier whose forms Jupiter Ammon and Jupiter of the Capitol took and who were seen with Olympias, mother of Alexander the Great, and Sempronia, mother of Scipio Africanus.' Alexander visited the shrine of Jupiter Ammon in the Libyan desert, and it was rumoured that he was actually the son of the god. In the same way it was rumoured that Jupiter of the Capitol in Rome was the father of Scipio Africanus, who saved Rome from the Carthaginians. *Highth*, 'principal man.'

511. *access*. Accent on last syllable.

517. wanton, 'frolicsome.'

522. Alludes to the story in the *Odyssey*, x, of the sailors of Odysseus turned into beasts by the enchantress, Circe.

525. *turret*, 'towering.' *enamelled*, 'shiny and variegated.'

529–530. "Either Satan directly moved the serpent's speech organs or he made the air vocal with some more direct impulse." (M.Y. Hughes.)

532 ff. Adam and Eve in Paradise were lords of the animals, and Satan's flattery takes off from this acknowledged and true lordship. He goes on to a sentiment common in the Cavalier lyric writers: that beauty should show, even flaunt, itself; as in Waller's "Go, lovely rose":

> Small is the worth
> Of beauty from the light retired:
> Bid her come forth,
> Suffer herself to be admired.

As in i, 501, where he talks of the "Sons of Belial, flown with insolence and wine" who wander forth after dark, Milton is thinking of the wilder young men who made the streets of London dangerous in the early days of

Charles II, so here he may be glancing at the lax sexual morals of Charles's court.

537. *awful*, 'awe-inspiring.'

538. As Satan knew that God had given man "dominion ... over every living thing," so he knew that "God created man in his own image." (*Genesis*, i.)

544. *shallow*, 'too imperceptive.'

546–548. Note the rhythm, broken and hesitant in the first line, betokening the present unsatisfactory state of affairs, and the confident rhythm that follows, betokening the triumph that Eve should enjoy.

549. *glozed*, 'talked speciously.' *his proem tuned*, 'framed his introduction.'

558. *The latter I demur*, 'I hesitate to accept the second notion.'

559. *reason* cannot here denote the quality of mind that distinguishes man from beast and allies him to the angels, but means merely good sense.

560. understand *to be* before *subtlest*.

563. *speakable of mute*, 'able to speak after being dumb.'

581–583. Snakes were imagined to like fennel and to suck the teats of sheep and goats.

599–600. *to degree/Of reason in my inward powers*: easy to understand but difficult to paraphrase, because *degree* can mean equally well *extent* and *level*, and in paraphrasing you have to opt for one or other meaning. But it is easy, and I believe correct, to understand both meanings at once.

601. *though to this shape retained* refers not to *speech* but to the serpent. Understand *I was* after *though*.

605. *middle*, 'air,' being between heaven and earth.

606. *fair*, used as a noun by Shakespeare too.

606 ff. Satan acts on the principle that if a person is susceptible to flattery at all he will swallow it in bulk. He proclaims that Eve sums up in herself the total virtue of the

universe and is its mistress. Observe too the dramatic quality of his words. There is a pause between *divine* and *semblance* caused by the ending of one line and the beginning of the next, and we can imagine Satan pausing to steal a glance at Eve's face to see how she is taking his words. And he leads up with other pauses and a kind of stealth to the resounding emphasis of the last line.

610. *importune*, 'importunate.'

612. *universal dame*, 'mistress of the universe.' *dame* retains the meaning of its Latin origin, *domina*. Compare the still current title, Dame of Sark.

613. *spirited*, 'spirit-possessed.'

615–616. Eve means that the serpent's excessive praise is unreasonable and hence makes her doubt his claim to have acquired reason from eating the fruit. Milton is true to nature in making Eve both repudiate flattery and be influenced by it.

622. *incorruptible* seems to imply that in Paradise the processes of growth and decay could be suspended for the convenience of man. Fruits would remain ripe waiting for new generations of men to pick them.

623. *to their provision*, 'to make use of the store provided for them.'

624. *birth*, 'produce.'

626. *ready*, 'open.'

627. *flat*, 'piece of level ground,' an archaic use of the word still surviving in its aquatic use—e.g., the flats and shoals of a river bed.

629. *blowing*, 'blossoming.' *balm*, 'balsam-tree.'

634. *wandering fire*, 'will-o'-the-wisp.'

635. *Compact of unctuous*, 'compounded of oily.'

643. *fraud*, interpreted by some editors in its Latin senses of crime and damage. But *credulous* in the next line makes the ordinary sense more likely. Satan led Eve into his toils of deception.

644–645. *tree/Of prohibition*, 'forbidden tree,' a Hebraism.

649. *credit*, 'credibility' or 'genuineness.' *rest*, the imperative.

653. *Sole daughter of his voice*, 'his sole command.' *the rest*, 'for the rest.'

664–665. *more bold/The tempter*. Milton shows much skill in making Satan more and more formidable and dominant as the temptation proceeds. His serpentine shape is splendid from the beginning, but at first he bows and fawns and assumes a "gentle dumb expression" (527). As he succeeds by his flattery in gaining Eve's attention and persuades her to follow him to the tree, "Hope elevates, and joy/Brightens his crest" (633–634). In other words he fawns no more but becomes a towering, dazzling figure. And now he puts on a grave and commanding dignity mixed with a feigned indignation that mankind should be in any way limited.

667. *New part puts on*, 'assumes a new character in the drama.'

668. *Fluctuates* has a physical meaning. Satan turns his body this way and that.

668–669. *in act raised*, 'dignified in his bodily action.'

669. *of*: we should now say *on*.

672. *since mute*. Milton is thinking of the oratory of Demosthenes and Cicero, which was largely political; and it is roughly true that the main impulse of English oratory had forsaken politics for the pulpit.

673. *in himself collected*, not just 'self-possessed' but 'with all his faculties assembled and ready for use.' *part*, *sc*. of his body.

674. *act*, 'action.' *audience*, not of course 'hearing' but 'notice' or 'attention.'

675. *Sometimes in highth*, still referring to the ancient orator. The normal technique of ancient oratory was to begin quietly and to work up to intense passion, but occa-

sionally the technique was to begin strikingly and passionately. *highth* means 'height of passion.'

680. *science,* 'knowledge.'

683. *highest agents,* 'active beings of the highest order.' These would seem to be the angels, those of the highest order included.

687. *to,* 'in addition to.'

689–690. Satan here states the kernel of what Milton meant by disobedience. It was a refusal to submit to the conditions of the state of life ordained for any creature by God.

690. *ventring,* 'venturing.'

694–695. *the pain/Of death denounced,* 'the proclamation of the penalty of death.' The use of *denounce* meaning *proclaim* is archaic, but *pain* meaning *penalty* still survives in the phrase *upon pain, of.*

698. *Of good, how just?* A much compressed phrase. Satan means: If the knowledge God forbids and punishes is of good, how can his act be just, for it cannot be wrong to know the good.

699. *why not known . . . ?* 'why should it not be known?'

701–702. Again, the language is much compressed. *of death* goes with *Your fear.* After *the fear* understand *of God.* There is no better explanation of these lines than that of Patrick Hume, Milton's earliest annotator (1695): "Justice is inseparable from the very being and essence of God, so that could he be unjust, he would be no longer God, and then neither to be obeyed nor feared; so that the fear of death, which does imply injustice in God, destroys itself, because God can as well cease to be, as cease to be just."

704. Note how Satan shifts his ground, knowing that his mind moves quicker than Eve's and that he can get her confused. He had suggested that God wanted Adam and Eve to eat the fruit to prove their courage. He now

says that God does not want them to do so because he grudges them the advantages they will get from the act. Though the two pleas are mutually exclusive they both point to the wisdom of eating the fruit; and Satan counts on Eve's heeding the advice while missing the inconsistency.

710–711. *since I as man,/Internal man,* 'since I have become like man, I mean like man within my serpentine exterior.' *gods,* 'angels.'

712. *of,* 'from being.'

713–714. Satan was the rival of God, trying to dispossess him. Milton reinforces this theme by making the Satanic motives parody the divine ones. Thus in Books Two and Ten Satan, Sin, and Death form a Trinity. Here he makes Satan speak in a kind of parody of St Paul. See 1 *Corinthians,* xv, 53, "For this corruptible must put on incorruption" and *Colossians,* iii, 9–10, "ye have put off the old man with his deeds and have put on the new man." In these and the next lines Satan seems to use *gods* in a deliberately muddled way, sometimes meaning angels, sometimes God, Father and Son, if not all together. He wants to put Eve's brain in a whirl.

718–719. *On our belief,* not 'to strengthen our already existing belief' but 'to create in us the belief.' When Satan seduced one third of the angels from their allegiance to God he cast doubt on God's having created them (v, 850 ff.); he now casts doubt on the natural superiority of any of the beings supposed to be man's superior, seeking to create in Eve a resentment at any kind of subordination.

722–725. Satan argues that no creator in his senses would have created an instrument for raising his creatures above the station in which he set them and have left them the power to use it. This implies that some agent other than the gods or God had enclosed knowledge of good and evil in thè tree. Satan does no more than imply; but what he does imply is that there is more than one creative force in the world, in other words the Manichaean heresy.

722. After *they* understand *produced.*

727–728. Another sudden shift of ground. Satan goes back to the position that there is one omnipotent creator and argues that omnipotence means total responsibility in him and none in the creature. What can it matter to omnipotence if one of his creatures knows more than before?

731. *import*, 'signify.'

732. *humane*, probably 'human.'

737. *impregned*, 'pregnant.'

742–743. *Inclinable . . . eye.* It is Eve who is inclined to touch and taste not her eye. If a strict grammatical explanation is required, I should say that *her eye* must be understood as *the eye of Eve* and that *inclinable* thus agrees with Eve.

746. *taste*, 'tasting.' *assay*, 'test.'

754. *while it infers*, 'provided it implies.'

756–757. These two lines explain the nature of *our want* in the line before.

758. *In plain*, sc. *words.*

768. *intellectual*, 'serving the intellect.'

771. *author unsuspect*, 'an authority, or source of knowledge, beyond suspicion.'

781. *eat*. 'ate.'

790. Milton here makes it clear that Eve's sin was more than the breaking of an order. It included the sin of pride, of aspiring to a state beyond the bounds set by nature.

792. *eating*, 'that she was eating.'

793. *boon*, an adjective, 'gay.'

795. *of*, 'among.'

796–797. *of operation blest/To sapience*, 'gifted with the

power to confer wisdom.' *infamed*, more likely 'mis-represented' or 'slandered' than 'without fame,' as Verity interprets.

800. Eve here is guilty of idolatry.

804–807. Eve has proved the apt pupil of Satan. She uses the word *gods* as he does and she adopts his assertion that they did not create the forbidden tree. See 713–714 and 722–735 above. *others*, "She means the gods, though, for decency's sake she names them not." (Newton).

807. *Experience*, 'experiment,' almost 'spirit of adventure.' After *owe* understand *a debt*.

808. *not following*, 'had I not followed.'

810. *access*. Accent on last syllable.

811. Eve is not sure of herself underneath. Just as in making her arch-blasphemy she had been diffident in calling God *others*, so now the word *secret*, just applied to *wisdom*, turns her mind abruptly to her misgivings.

812. *to see*, 'for seeing.'

815–816. *safe with all his spies/About him*, 'safely out of the way and unsuspicious because relying on his bodyguard.' Eve pictures God as a tyrant. For *safe* in this sense see Shakespeare, *Tempest*, III, i, 19–21, where Miranda says to Ferdinand, "My father/Is hard at study; pray now, rest yourself;/He's safe for these three hours."

823. *more equal* cannot at the present date fail to remind one of Orwell's now famous, "All animals are equal, but some are more equal than others." The next lines show that Eve did wish to be "more equal" in the Orwellian sense.

825. Eve has indeed adopted the Satanic doctrine but, if Satan applied it to himself and God, she applies it here to herself and her husband.

829. *enjoying* probably goes with *her* and will mean that she will enjoy Adam's love, while Eve is extinct.

835. *done*, 'having been done.'

837. *sciential*, 'productive of knowledge.'

845. *divine of*, 'prophetic of.'

846. *measure*, 'beat' (of his heart).

853-854. 'Her expression of self-excuse served as a pre-
liminary in itself and served also to introduce a verbal
defence.' Milton might have had in mind a dumb-show
like that in the play within *Hamlet*, which showed by
act and gesture what was to follow in words.

855. *with bland words at will*, 'able to summon up persuasive
words.'

864. *tasted*, 'when tasted.'

872. *to admiration*, 'in a marvellous way.' Compare *to perfection*.

877-878. A quickly improvised lie, to impress Adam.

887. *Distemper* means a disordered state of body or mind
and here it almost means fever. But the word had different connotations in Milton's day from what it has in
ours. It referred in its basic sense to the upsetting of the
balance of the bodily humours on whose proper tem-
pering health depended.

893. The roses faded in sympathy with Adam's horror,
thus fortelling the effect that Eve's crime will have on
nature.

899. *amiable*, not so tepid a word as it has become since
Milton's day but more like *lovely*.

901. *devote*, 'doomed.'

909. *converse*. Accent on second syllable.

910. "These words of Adam imply that the mere imagina-
tion of losing Eve had already converted the sweets of
Paradise into the horrors of a desolate wilderness."
(Thyer.)

919. *remediless*. Accent on second syllable.

921. *presumed*, 'ventured upon,' an archaic use of the word.
But Milton may have wanted the reader to think at the same
time of the Latin *praesumere*, meaning *to anticipate*. Not
only did Eve venture upon the deed but she got in first.

923. *it*, 'the daring act,' understood from *Last dared* in the line before. *coveting*, the verbal noun.

924. *sacred* has the sense of the Latin *sacer*, 'dedicated.'

925. *Much more to taste*, 'much more peril have you provoked by daring to taste.'

927. *so*, 'even so'.

928. *fact*, 'deed.'

929. *foretasted fruit*, an absolute construction.

933. *gains to live*. Here *gains* could be either transitive or intransitive; and the meaning would be either 'obtains an existence' or 'benefits so as to live.' *as man*. Adam does not mean that the serpent had acquired human form; he means that his intelligence has risen from the bestial to the human level.

935. *tasting*, 'if we taste.'

937. By *gods* Eve probably means the highest grades of angel, contrasted with the lower grades, the simple angels or demi-gods.

945. *Not well conceived of God*: a loose apposition of the typically Miltonic kind. We must understand something like 'a way of behaving,' and the sense would continue 'not to be thought of on God's part.'

952. *However*. By this word Adam betrays that he has small confidence in his arguments and he goes on to give his real reason for adding his own disobedience to Eve's.

953. *Certain*, 'resolved.'

961. *trial* bears the now obsolete sense of *evidence* or *proof*.

962. *example high*. According to the universally accepted Renaissance theory the aim of the highest poetry was to instruct through the example, tragedy exhibiting what was to be shunned, epic exhibiting what was to be imitated. Milton is grimly ironical in making Eve speak of Adam's resolve to defy God's command as if it were a typical act of epic heroism.

963. *short*, 'since I am short.'

965 ff. Eve in her infatuate excitement jumps from one thought to another, but, though full of parentheses, her words are clear enough.

974. *Direct or by occasion*, 'directly or indirectly.'

975. *trial*. See 961.

977. *ensue* is here used transitively.

980. *oblige thee with a fact*, 'make you responsible for a deed.'

981. *chiefly assured*, again the typical loose apposition. The connection of thought seems to be: 'I should be willing to make such a sacrifice chiefly because I have just been assured . . .'

984. *event*, 'issue.'

986-987. The irony of Eve's depreciating her past happy experiences can only be grasped by recalling the lovely and passionate descriptions, earlier in the poem, of the beauties of Paradise and of married bliss among them. She is terribly far gone in hectic infatuation.

990 ff. Note the beautiful and tragic simplicity, contrasted with Eve's headlong speech, with which Milton describes the committing of the primal human sin.

992. *of choice*. The rhythm suggests an emphasis on the words, an emphasis taken up in lines 998-999. While Eve's sin had been mainly in the realm of the *understanding*, Adam's was in that of the *will*. The serpent had thrown dust in her eyes, but Adam saw clearly. See note on 239.

1002. *muttering thunder*. Either this is an absolute construction meaning 'while the thunder muttered'; or *muttering* is transitive and the *sad drops*, representing the cloud from which they fell, muttered the thunder.

1018. *elegant*, 'discriminating.' *sapience*, 'wisdom.'

1019. 'since we equate the word *savour* with the meanings both of good taste and of wisdom.' Adam makes and explains a rather silly pun in accord with the irresponsible mood that now possesses him.

1024–1026. Of these lines I wrote: "Milton's grim humour never showed more dramatic power than in these lines. We can hear Eve's hectic, infatuate giggles at Adam's words."

1033. *bounty of*, 'through the virtue of,' 'thanks to.'

1034. *toy*, 'caress.' The lines that follow, describing the pair's sudden and unceremonious fit of love, should be compared with the passage about their wedding-bower in iv, 689 ff. In the earlier passage Milton compares the dignity and ceremony of married love with the 'casual fruition' of harlots. The effect of the forbidden fruit on Adam and Eve is to make them forget the ceremony of married love and to indulge in a sudden fit of lust, in fact in the sort of casual fruition that Milton condemns. Spenser created a similar contrast in describing his Bower of Bliss and Garden of Adonis in the *Faerie Queene*. See C. S. Lewis's *Allegory of Love*, chapter on Spenser.

1037 ff. The insertion of this dulcet description of the flowery bank seems strangely inept just here. Possibly Milton meant us to compare the flowers' innocence with the human pair's corruption but, if so, he gives no indication that this was his intention.

1040. *asphodel*, probably here the mythical flower that grew in the Greek Elysium and hence appropriate in Paradise.

1046 ff. Milton speaks here in terms of the physiology of his day, and *spirits* has a technical meaning. The spirits were created by the grosser humours and were the executive in man's microcosm. For a more detailed account of their operation see my *Elizabethan World Picture*, p. 65.

1049. *grosser sleep*, intended to contrast with Adam's light sleep in his time of innocence: "for his sleep/Was airy light, from pure digestion bred/And temperate vapours bland." (V, 3–5.)

1050. *unkindly*, 'unnatural.'

1054. *innocence*. Milton explains in the lines that follow what he meant by the innocence from which Adam and Eve had fallen. It is more than the passive state of lack of sinful feelings and implies positive confidence in the rightness of their state of mind and of their actions.

1055. *knowing ill* means the experience of evil thoughts within them rather than the power to discriminate between good and ill. Adam and Eve had never lacked that power, and it was the new experience of evil thoughts that brought with it the new feeling of shame.

1058. *Shame*, a personification; *he* refers to this Shame personified. Shame's robe or covering was shame, and this revealed more than it concealed.

1059 ff. The story of Samson's losing his strength through his wife's cutting off his hair while he slept is told in *Judges*, xvi, 6–21. As Samson of the tribe of Dan woke to find his strength gone, so Adam and Eve woke to find their innocence gone.

1060–1061. Accent *Herculean* on the second syllable, *Philistean* on the third. The Authorised Version reads *Delilah* with the accent traditionally on the second syllable. Milton's form is *Dalilah* or *Dalila* with the accent on the first syllable.

1068. *worm*, 'serpent.'

1069. *true* probably agrees with *voice* and not with *worm*. It is the serpent's voice or words that were true in foretelling man's fall or death and false in foretelling the glorious resurrection from such fall. Milton may be referring back to Satan's words in 713 ff., "So ye shall die perhaps etc."

1079. *last*, not of course *last in time*, but *culminating* or *extreme*. The Latin *extremus* bears both senses. And *first* correspondingly means *subsidiary*.

1083. *earthly*, 'earthly nature.'

1085. People in Milton's, as in Shakespeare's, day were

acutely conscious of man's middle position between the
angels and the beasts. Milton here makes Adam in his
shame shrink from his higher self that approaches the
angels and long to identify himself with the beasts.

1090. *them*, the dazzling heavenly shapes.

1091. *as in bad plight*, a Latinism (*ut in* etc.), excusable for its
terseness and meaning 'in view of our bad plight.'

1094. *obnoxious*, 'liable.' *seen*, 'to be seen.'

1101 ff. Milton's fig-tree with its wilderness of parent- and
daughter-trees and its broad leaves derives from several
botanical facts and literary sources. Botanically the tree is
a confusion of the Indian banyan, which propagates itself
in the way described, and the plantain or banana, which
has large leaves. The literary accounts go back to Pliny's
Natural History, but Milton used most obviously the
account given by John Gerard in his *Herbal*, the most
famous of Elizabethan books on botany, published in
1597, for some of his phrases actually duplicate Gerard's.
Malabar is the south-western coast of India and Decan
the district around Goa. This is part of Gerard's account
of the Indian fig:

> The ends of the branches hang down and touch the
> ground, where they take root, and grow in such sort that
> those twigs become great trees; and these, being grown up
> unto like greatness, do cast their branches or twiggy ten-
> drils unto the earth, where they likewise take hold and root.
> By means whereof it cometh to pass that of one tree is
> made a great wood or desert of trees, which the Indians
> do use for coverture against the extreme heat of the sun.
> Some likewise use them for pleasure, cutting down by a
> direct line a long walk or as it were a vault through the
> thickest part, from which they also cut certain loopholes or
> windows in some places, to the end to receive thereby the
> fresh cool air that entreth thereat, as also for light that they
> may see their cattle that feed thereby. From which vault

or close walk doth rebound an admirable echo. The first
or mother of this wood is hard to be known from the
children.

1111. *Amazonian targe*, 'kind of shield used by the Amazons.' These shields were shaped like a crescent. Milton
got the resemblance of the leaves of the banyan to the
Amazons' shield from Pliny and Gerard but he may have
used the word *Amazonian* in reference to Eve's having
taken the lead in an unnatural way, for the warrior life
of the Amazons was something contrary to nature.

1117. *cincture*, 'wrapping.'

1121–1131. There is much traditional lore, such as I have
described in my *Elizabethan World Picture*, contained in
these lines. It was a commonplace to put the human
passions in terms of storms and upheavals in the physical
world. In 1125 Milton refers to the traditional comparison
of man's mind to a kingdom, *region* retaining its original
meaning of an area under the rule of a king. This comparison occurs in a famous passage in Shakespeare's
Julius Caesar. Brutus, troubled in conscience over his
share in the conspiracy, soliloquises:

> Between the acting of a dreadful thing
> And the first motion, all the interim is
> Like a phantasma or a hideous dream.
> The genius and the mortal instruments
> Are then in council; and the state of man,
> Like to a little kingdom, suffers then
> The nature of an insurrection.

The understanding and the will were the two divisions of
the supreme human faculty, the reason; and when (1129)
Milton talks of the sensual appetite working from beneath he is referring to the current psychology that
placed the different human motions in different parts of
the body The lowest part, governed by the liver, was the

seat of man's lowest instincts. For *distempered* (1131) see note on 887. *i.e. Disordered state, humours out of proportion.*

1132. *and altered style* agrees most likely with Adam and means 'changed in manner of address.'

1140. *approve*, 'make proof of.' Adam refers to Eve's plea (335) that virtue has no standing unless put to the test.

1141. *owe*, 'own.'

1163. *Is this the love* ... ? Adam speaks brokenly in his passion. His full meaning is: 'is this the love you promised me?' but he breaks off and begins another question. Adam refers to Eve's speech beginning 961.

1164. *mine*, 'my love.'

1164–1165. *expressed/Immutable*, 'which was shown to be immutable.'

1169. Understand *as being* before *not*.

1175. *confidence*, 'overconfidence.'

1189. *contest*. Accent on the last syllable.

Book X

1. *heinous* probably means 'motivated by hate' and not in the modern sense, 'worthy of being hated.' *despiteful*, then, will mean 'motivated by envy.'

10. *complete*, 'sufficient in itself.'

11. *whatever*, 'any.'

16. *manifold*. Milton agreed with the current theology in thinking that the eating of the fruit incurred the sin not only of disobedience but of such evils as gluttony, uxor-iousness, excessive ambition.

18. *angelic guards*, Gabriel and his attendants, who figure prominently in Book Four.

21–28. These lovely lines show both the impossible nature of Milton's theme and his triumph in creating poetry nevertheless. We are incapable of combining pity with perfect bliss or of imagining such a combination in a superior order of being. Yet this is what Milton wants us to do and in a way pretends he can do: on the face of it an act of hypocrisy. What he in fact does is to render with the simplest means and the utmost delicacy a recognizable state of the human mind: the state of a man experienced and settled in temper, saddened by the spectacle of human ills but not broken by them; a state perfectly apt to the angels as humanly conceivable, however in-applicable to the abstract demand of their perfect bliss. What is true of these lines is true of Milton's total theme.

28–31. *Accountable* is taken by the best commentators to go with *vigilance*, and the meaning would be "They, approaching the throne, hastened to make their vigilance, which had been the best they were capable of, appear sufficient for the account they were expected to render; and they vindicated their conduct." But this interpretation demands the rather queer understanding of *going* before *towards* and a distortion of the natural word order violent even for Milton. It also demands a rhythm which strikes me as unMiltonic. I prefer to make *accountable* agree with *they* and to interpret the lines thus : 'Knowing that they were liable to be called to account, they hastened towards the throne, in order to make evident that they had watched with the utmost care; and they vindicated their conduct."

33. The thunderings of the Christian God are derived from *Revelation*, but Milton liked to think that he continued the tradition of his epic predecessors, Homer and Virgil, whose pagan chief deity thundered from Olympus.

38. *Foretold*, 'having been warned.'

40. *speed*, 'succeed.'

45. *moment*, used in its Latin sense of a stress influencing the decision of a pair of scales. *impulse*. Accent on the last syllable.

48. *rests*, 'remains.' *pass*, intransitive, 'be passed.'

49. *death denounced that day*, 'the proclamation of the doom of death made on the day the crime was committed.'

54. Verity understands *has been* after *bounty*; and the meaning would be, " Justice will insist on acting, since Adam and Eve scorned the bounty offered them in Eden by seeking to enlarge it into things forbidden." But it is simpler to take *scorned* as a participle agreeing with *bounty* and to interpret: "They cannot escape justice as they could escape an unwanted gift by merely refusing it."

59. *colleague*, probably a verb, 'to join in alliance with.' Accent on last syllable. *sending*, 'since I send.'

62. *destined man himself*, 'destined to be very man.'

65. Only the two other persons of the deity could bear the full blaze of the Father's presence. In iii, 372 ff., the angels hymn the Father as

> inaccessible but when thou shad'st
> The full blaze of thy beams, and, through a cloud
> Drawn round about thee like a radiant shrine
> Dark with excessive light thy skirts appear.

full, 'fully.'

66–67. The interpretation depends on what meaning we give to *expressed*. If we give it the modern sense, the passage means that the Son plainly gave forth as much brilliance as the Father. But *express* in Milton's day could mean "be the image of," and the passage could mean that the Son gave back or reflected the full brilliance of the Father. Behind Milton's words is Hebrews, i, 3, "who being the brightness of his glory and the express [*i.e.* "exact"] image of his person . . . sat down on the right hand of the majesty on high."

77. *derived*, 'diverted.'

78–79. *as may illustrate most/Them fully satisfied*, 'as may best adorn justice and mercy while fully satisfying their claims.' Accent *illustrate* on the second syllable.

83. *Convict*, 'convicted' with accent on last syllable.

84. *Conviction*, 'formal proof of guilt.' This is superfluous in view of the serpent's flight.

86. *collateral*, 'parallel.'

89. *coast*, 'surrounding region.'

91. Time is here personified. He measures time by the beat of his wings, this being the smallest unit of measure. But he cannot count God's speed in his journey to earth, for it is less than this smallest unit of measure. *Minute* means, not sixty seconds, but a tiny fraction of time.

92. *cadence* keeps its original Latin sense of 'decline.'

93. *noon*, 'highest point in heaven.'

95. Milton derived God's visiting Adam and Eve "in the cool of the day" from *Genesis*, but his making the coolness of evening correspond to the Son's "coolness," or freedom from anger, is quite typical of his age. In Milton's day nature existed less as an independent set of phenomena than as a set of emblems of human states of mind. The correspondence is much more than what Verity calls "not a very happy play on words."

106. *obvious* has its Latin meaning of 'standing in the way' or 'being there to meet.' The whole line means, 'whereas formerly you did your duty of meeting and welcoming me without being told.'

112. *apparent*, 'evident.'

115. *Whence*, ' rom the midst of which passions.'

118. *revile*, revilement.'

120. *still*, 'always.'

139. *acceptable*. Accent on first and third syllables.

141. *whatever in itself*, 'whatever its essential nature.'

141–142. *what she did . . . deed*. Here is redundance, and one of these is, strictly, unnecessary. But the redundance conveys the tone of conversation and Adam's confusion well enough.

149. *made of thee*, 'whom God created from your rib.'

154. *well seemed*, 'showed to advantage.'

156. *person*, a dramatic metaphor. To sustain his proper character in the drama of life Adam had to be Eve's superior.

165 ff. Modern readers will not sympathise with Milton's attempt to justify the punishment of the serpent, now freed from the intrusion of Satan. Milton seems to argue that the serpent ought not to have allowed itself to be used by Satan, but without persuading the reader- Milton's trouble was that he had to follow *Genesis*, where the mere animal initiates the temptation, un-

prompted by any devil, and justly incurs punishment. But, for his own poetic purposes, he also chose to follow a later tradition which made Satan use the serpent as his mouthpiece and which made God's doom pronounced on the serpent also signify, in allegorical terms, God's doom pronounced on Satan and Christ's victory over him. Milton justifies God's punishing the serpent, as just explained, and adds that for the moment Adam does not know (and need not know) that God's words extend farther. Later in the book (1030–1036) Adam remembers God's words and gives them their additional meaning. If we find Milton's careful explanations strained, we should remember the sanctity of every phrase of the Bible in Milton's day and his need not to violate a single detail of it.

165. *unable* qualifies *serpent*.

166. *on him*, Satan.

167. *polluted* could be either an active verb having Satan as the subject or a passive participle qualifying the serpent. I prefer the latter and take *unable . . . polluted . . . accurs'd* as a series all applied to the serpent.

171. *Nor alter'd his offence.* *Man* in the previous line is generic and refers to Adam and Eve. Whether it was the mere serpent or Satan speaking through him made no difference to the nature of their crime.

171–172. Milton plays on the ideas of *last* and *first*. Though Satan was first in crime God made his doom, addressed to the serpent in the first instance, apply only last to Satan.

179–181. As one would expect, this mysterious prophecy in *Genesis* was given an allegorical meaning. Satan's hostility to Eve, already manifested, shall continue and extend to her descendants, that is to all mankind, Jesus included. The bruising of the heel of the descendant, Jesus, or descendants of Eve signified the tribulation to which Satan was allowed to submit them. But, in revenge, he would suffer a more deadly wound, in his head, through Christ's triumphant resurrection and ascension and through the parallel triumph of the faithful. Milton adopted this current allegory.

183. As Christ was thought of as the second Adam (see 1 *Corinthians*, xv, 21) so his mother was thought of as the second Eve, able to correct the faults of her ancestress.

184–189. To understand these lines, as Milton's contemporaries would have found no difficulty in doing, the modern reader must recall many references to Scripture. The fall of Satan is recorded in *Luke*, x, 18; but the context is also important. Jesus had sent out seventy disciples with power to heal and cast out devils; and they returned to him rejoicing that they had indeed been able to exercise this second power. Whereupon Jesus said: "I beheld Satan as lightning fall from heaven. Behold, I give unto you power to tread on serpents and scorpions and over all the power of the enemy." Doubtless, it was this reference to treading on serpents that made Milton connect the whole passage in Luke with the bruising of the serpent's head in *Genesis*. The title of Satan as prince of the air comes from *Ephesians*, ii, 2. The air, the devils' realm, was the space between the sphere of the moon and the earth. According to the traditional cosmology the universe from the moon upwards was immutable, and Satan had no sway there. Mutability began below the moon; and there Satan was free to operate. Lines 186–187 come straight from *Colossians*, ii, 15, where Christ, "having spoiled principalities and powers, made a show of them openly, triumphing over them in" his cross. Milton's contemporaries took the verse to mean something like, "having disarmed Satan and all his subordinate devils of their power, exposed them to the contempt of

God and the good angels in his triumph over them."
And this is likely to be the meaning of Milton's words.
187–188 come from St Paul's interpretation of a passage
in *Psalms*, lxiii, 18: "Thou hast ascended on high, thou
hast led captivity captive." St Paul, quoting the passage
in *Ephesians*, iv, 8, applied it to Christ's ascension and to
his triumph over Satan and his powers.

210. *denounced*, 'proclaimed.'

215. The episode of Christ's washing his disciples' feet is
told in *John*, xiii, 5.

217–218. Milton shows here that he is puzzled by the statement in *Genesis*, iii, 21, that "unto Adam also and to his
wife did the Lord God make coats of skins and clothed
them." Where did the skins come from? Most easily
from the animals in Paradise. But, so far, death had not
entered there and, when it did, it would do so more
fittingly through the agency of Satan, Sin, and Death, the
infernal Trinity described in Book One and shortly
to appear in the present book. So Milton, though hesitant because of its zoological shakiness, insinuates the
possibility that some animal may have shed its skin after
the manner of snakes.

220. *outward*. Understand *nakedness* from the next line.

222. See *Isaiah*, lxi, 10, "The Lord hath covered me with
the robe of righteousness."

230 ff. For Satan's encounter with Sin and Death, who sit
one opposite the other ("in counterview") within Hell-
gate, see ii, 648 ff. Satan there finds that Death is his son
by Sin, who is also his own daughter.

245. *this deep*, Hell.

246–248. Milton here writes in terms of the old medieval
science, based on Aristotle, which tended to animate
natural objects, as in the doctrine of the Intelligences that
guided the spheres. See H. Butterfield, *The Origins of
Modern Science*, 7: "A universe constructed on the

mechanics of Aristotle had the door half-way open for
spirits already; it was a universe in which unseen hands
had to be in constant operation, and sublime Intelligences
had to roll the planetary spheres around. Alternatively,
bodies had to be endowed with souls and aspirations,
with a 'disposition' to certain kinds of motion.''

256. *unagreeable*, 'inappropriate' as well as 'unpleasant.'
found, 'build.'

260. *intercourse*, 'two-way traffic.'

261. *transmigration*, 'permanent emigration.'

263. *instinct*. Accent on last syllable.

264. *meagre*, 'lean.'

266. *err*, 'mistake.'

267. *draw*, *i.e.*, into my nostrils.

273. The commentators give several parallels in literature
to the notion that birds of prey have a premonition of a
coming battle from which they can profit. The notion
was plainly a commonplace. One of the most apt parallels is from Beaumont and Fletcher's *Beggar's Bush*:
"'tis said of vultures,/They scent a field fought and so
smell the carcases/By many hundred miles."

277. *designed*, 'marked out.'

279. *feature*, 'form.' See Shakespeare, *Henry VIII*, iii, 2,
50: "She is a gallant creature and complete/In mind and
feature."

281. *Sagacious of*, 'able to scent.'

282 ff. To grasp the full import of the splendid description
that follows one must know that it parodies the description earlier in the poem (vii, 210–242) of the Son and
Spirit going out from Heaven to create the world from
chaos. As a parody it contains something of the grotesque, a kind of monstrous grandeur. Here are some of
the parallels between the two descriptions. The divine
Trinity is matched by the infernal Trinity of Satan, Sin,
and Death; and it is the second and third in each who do

see also
Virgil .
Lucan

the work. The Holy Spirit broods like a dove over the abyss; Sin and Death hover over it like birds of prey. The Spirit creates through warmth and growth and purges away the intractable dregs. Death solidifies his causeway by chill and petrifaction, and the solid and slimy materials he uses are those very 'cold infernal dregs, adverse to life' which the Spirit had rejected. Generally, the second passage is violent and excessive where the first passage is easy, though vast, and serene.

283. Milton described Chaos in the second book of his poem. It was a confused heap of the elements of creation.

284. *diverse*, 'in different directions.'

288. *shoaling*, 'heaping into a shoal or bank.'

289. *adverse*, 'from opposite directions.'

290. *Cronian*, 'Arctic.'

291. *the imagined way*. Man dreamt of and tried to find a northern sea-passage from west to east through the Arctic Ocean north of Siberia to China.

292. *Petsora*, a gulf of the Arctic Ocean in the north of Russia in Europe, issuing at a point opposite the islands of Nova Zembla.

293. *Cathaian*. The travellers who reached China overland called the country Cathay. And they thought of it as a different country from the China long known by the sea route from India. Milton seems to have kept the two countries distinct and by Cathay means northern China. The wealth of Cathay was proverbial. *aggregated*, 'accumulated.'

293 ff. From the confused elements, hot, cold, wet, dry, Death chose those adverse to life, the cold and dry and, as Neptune with his trident once collected the matter that formed the island of Delos in the Aegean sea, solidified them with a touch of his petrifying sceptre. Then, as Jupiter fixed the floating island of Delos to the sea bottom to serve as the birthplace of Apollo and Diana,

Death tied in part of the heap he had made to plant the foundation of his bridge near Hell-gate. What he did not use for this foundation he moulded with the slimy matter the two had collected (see 286) and made immovable with his mere look, as the Gorgon, killed by Perseus, was reputed to turn whatever looked at her to stone. By the same process Sin and Death, having attached the matter they had collected to the solid mass of Hell, prolonged it across the gulf of Chaos to the hard exterior of the universe.

297–298. Commentators have found the notion of binding something by an insubstantial look and by very substantial slime simultaneously too violent to be admissible; and indeed one is reminded of Lewis Carroll in the *Hunting of the Snark*: "They sought him with thimbles,/ They sought him with care.' And some editors have tried to escape the difficulty by altering the punctuation. But Milton's grotesqueness here was intentional.

298. *asphaltic*, 'bituminous.'

302–303. *wall*: the solid, outer shell of the universe enclosing the different spheres. *fenceless*, 'defenceless.'

305. *inoffensive*, 'unobstructed.' The Latin *offendere* means basically to strike against.

307 ff. Xerxes, king of Persia, invading Greece through Asia Minor, made a bridge of boats across the Bosphorus for his armies to pass over to Europe. When a storm destroyed the bridge, he is said to have ordered the waves to be beaten. Herodotus is the source for this famous legend.

308. *Susa*, Xerxes's winter residence in Persia, whose citadel was supposed to have been built by Memnon, son of Tithonus and Aurora.

313. *Pontifical*. Milton uses the word in its literal Latin sense of 'bridge-making.' But its usual meaning was 'episcopal' or 'papal,' the Latin *pontifex* meaning a priest.

Milton may well be taking a stab at the Roman church; but his main aim is to develop, through the strange use of the word, a sense of monstrosity.

315. The journey of Satan through Chaos to the outer shell of the universe is the subject of the last part of Book Two.

317. *to the outside* can be taken in two ways. Either it can refer to Satan, and *to* will mean *onto*; or it can refer to the bridge and be connected with *they brought the work* in line 312. The second explanation leads on well to what follows.

321 ff. The point where the new bridge ended was near the opening in the outer shell of the universe giving access to the spheres and finally to the earth at their centre. It was by this route that the angels had been in the habit of visiting the human pair. There were thus two roads, the one from Heaven to this point on the outside of the universe and the one thence into the universe. The bridge from Hell made a third road. The point is that now the earth is exposed equally to the good offices of Heaven and the evil offices of Hell.

322. *left*, because the left is the unlucky side. In pictures of the Last Judgment the damned are always on the left side.

326. *To Paradise first tending*, 'making Paradise the first aim of their journey.'

327. *likeness*, 'the disguise.'

328–329. The point of this piece of astronomy is that by choosing this position for his voyage upwards to the exit from the universe Satan would have the earth between him and the sun and escape the notice of Uriel, the angel of the sun, with whom he had had trouble before (see end of Book Four).

332. *after Eve seduced*: a Latinism, meaning 'after Eve had been seduced' or 'after the seduction of Eve.' The advantage of it is that it saves two words; and one of the

warrants of poetry is its superior conciseness. *unminded*, 'unnoticed.'

335. *though all unweeting*. At first sight *though all unweeting* might appear illogical, for Eve's unawareness would not make her *less* likely to urge on her husband the trick Satan played on her; rather the reverse. Nor are things made better by making *unweeting* go with *husband*. So the phrase should be confined to the relations between Satan and Eve. She seconded (or repeated) Satan's act, but, unlike him, she did not do so guilefully.

339. *not hoping etc.*, 'not hoping to escape ultimate judgment but hoping only to avoid immediate punishment.'

344-345. *which understood/Not instant*, 'and when he understood that this was not instant.' Again Latinisms, making for conciseness.

345-346. *with joy/And tidings fraught*, 'filled with joyful tidings.'

348. *pontifice*, 'bridge-structure.'

349. The monosyllable *met* comes abruptly and surprisingly at the beginning of this line, expressing the abrupt surprise of the meeting. *who*, understand *those* before it.

364. *Such fatal consequence*, 'such a bond, decreed by fate.'

370. *fortify*, 'make, *i.e.* build, solidly.'

372. *virtue*, 'courage.'

374. *odds*, 'advantage.'

375. *foil*, 'defeat.'

378. Accent *own* and the penultimate syllable of *alienated*, and the line reads easily. *doom*, 'decree.'

380. *empyreal*, 'celestial.'

381. *quadrature*, 'square-shaped dominion,' as described in *Revelation*, xxi, 16: "The city lieth four-square." *orbicular*, 'round.'

382. *try*, 'find by trial.'

386-387. The name, Satan, means 'adversary' or 'antagonist.'

388-389. *Of all/The infernal empire,* 'of all the inhabitants of Hell.'

390. 'have matched one triumphal act with another.'

391. *Mine with this glorious work,* 'my success in tempting Adam and Eve with the bridge you have built.'

406. *all,* 'entirely.'

413. *planets, planet-struck:* a rather frigid playing with ideas. The planets were about to have influence, good and bad, on human affairs, and the word, *planet-struck* came to mean 'blasted' or 'withered.' Sin and Death had on the planets the blasting effect that it became the planets' special property to exercise; the planets were on this occasion hoist with their own petard. *Eclipse,* 'dimming' or 'loss of splendour.'

415. *causey,* 'causeway.'

416. Milton means that Chaos protested indignantly against having been divided and bridged; once again a Latin construction making for conciseness.

423. The run of this line is not at first sight clear. Read "fár to th'inlánd."

425. *called* refers to Lucifer not to Pandemonium.

426. *Of:* we now talk of an allusion *to. star to Satan paragoned:* the star with which Lucifer was equated (*paragoned*) was the planet Venus, the morning and evening star, on the authority of *Isaiah,* xiv, 12, "How art thou fallen from Heaven. O Lucifer, son of the morning."

427. *the grand,* 'the members of the infernal council' (see Book Two).

428. *solicitous,* 'anxious as to.'

429. *sent,* 'on his mission.'

430. *observed,* 'obeyed.'

432. In Milton's day Astracan, on the lower Volga, was near the frontier of Russia and the kingdom of the Tartars.

433. *Retires.* We should understand "leaving all waste" from the next line.

433–434. *Bactrian Sophi from the horns/Of Turkish crescent,* 'the Persian Shah, retiring from the crescent formation of the Turkish army.' Bactria was one of the chief Persian provinces. Persian and Turkey were often at war in the seventeenth century.

435. *Aladule,* the mountainous part of Armenia.

436. *Tauris,* now Tabriz. *Casbeen,* now Kasbin, formerly capital of Persia, south of the Caspian Sea.

438. *reduced* has its basic Latin sense and means 'led back' or 'withdrawn.'

441. Satan first passed through the guards outside Pandemonium; he then entered by the door and made his way, invisible, to the throne within.

445. *state,* 'canopy.'

449. This theatrical act of Satan illustrates the streak of vulgarity which Milton gave to his character.

451. *permissive,* 'permitted.'

454. *aspect,* 'gaze.' Accent on the last syllable.

456. The infernal council had been occupying another room away from the great assembly hall.

457. *dark divan,* 'secret council.' *Divan* is the Arabic and Turkish for supreme council.

460. Satan repeats a formula of address that God has used before the revolt of the bad angels.

461–462. What were hitherto but nominal (though legitimate) titles have now become actual.

471. Chaos was *unreal* because it was ever changing and had no significant form.

475. *uncouth,* 'unknown.'

477. *unoriginal,* 'having no known origin.'

479. *uproar.* Accent on last syllable.

480. *Protesting fate supreme,* 'urging as an obstacle the hostility of supreme fate.' *Protest* could in Milton's day also

mean 'to invoke as witness;' and the words have been
also explained as "calling upon fate as a witness against
my proceedings." Before *thence* understand from line 469
long were to tell.

484. *exile*. Accent on last syllable.

488. *Offended* bears not the modern sense but one nearer its
root meaning in Latin: 'caused to stumble or trip up' or,
as we should say, 'caught out by it.'

494. *he* refers back to the creator in line 486.

513. *supplanted* is used in its original, physical, sense of
'throw a man off his feet.'

515. *reluctant*, 'striving to resist.'

520. *accessories*. Accent on first and penultimate syllables.

521. *riot*, 'disorder' or 'revolt,' referring not to the devils'
original revolt but to Satan's upsetting of the order of
things in corrupting the human pair.

523. 'with monsters intertwined head and tail.'

524–526. Milton shows here that he knew the medieval
bestiaries, which describe all kind of fabulous beasts. The
amphisbaena was a snake with a head at each end. *Hydrus*
was a water-snake. *Ellops* means mute. *Dipsas* caused in
those it stung an unquenchable thirst. Those who want to
know about the amazing qualities of most of the snakes
Milton listed can consult *The Book of Beasts*, a medieval
bestiary translated and annotated by T. H. White,
165–194.

526–527. Perseus cut off the head of the Gorgon, Medusa,
in Africa. As he returned with her head, it dropped blood
over Libya and the drops turned into snakes.

528. *Ophiusa*, an island of the Balearic group. Libya and this
island were popularly supposed to abound in snakes.

529. After *than* understand *the one*.

529–531. In classical mythology, after the flood had sub-
sided, the slime that remained, acted on by the sun, bred
various monsters, among which was the great snake,

Python, on the site of Delphi. Apollo killed Python with his arrows. The best known account of this famous myth is in Ovid, *Metamorphoses*, i, 434 ff.

534. *All yet left*, all the devils that were not inside Pandemonium.

535. *in station*, 'on guard.' *just array*, 'regular military formation.'

536. *sublime* bears its original Latin sense of 'elevated' or 'uplifted.' One could almost paraphrase 'on tiptoe.' Milton creates a wonderful grotesque picture of the devils outside Pandemonium, still in their own shapes, awaiting the triumphal exit of the rest, led by Satan and his peers, and seeing instead a mob of varied and hideous snakes emerge.

540. *sympathy* bears more than its usual modern sense and means 'common suffering.'

541. *changing*, 'changing into' or 'becoming.'

546. *exploding*, not 'explosive,' but, according to the Latin sense of the word, indicating the kind of hiss used to drive an actor off the stage, the opposite of the applause that Satan had expected.

557. *Though to delude them sent*, a much compressed phrase, meaning 'though they knew that the trees and their fruit were sent to delude them.'

560. *curled*, 'made curly.' *Megaera* was one of the Furies, and these had snaky locks.

561-562. The legend of the Dead Sea (*bituminous lake*) apples that tempted the sight but dissolved into ashes at the first touch goes back to Josephus, the Jewish historian (first century A.D.), and was repeated by some of the medieval writers of travel, including Mandeville. Sodom and Gomorrah were near the Dead Sea.

565. *with gust*, usually explained as 'with relish' but more apt if explained as 'by tasting.' The mere satisfying of

thirst was what mattered to the devils, not the doing so with relish.

566. *the offended taste*, 'the taste, taking offense.'

568. *drugged*, 'nauseated.'

570–572. *triumphed*, 'triumphed over.' The devils are contrasted with man; they thought that they had triumphed over man on account of his *single* lapse only to find that they fell *repeatedly* themselves. The whole episode of the devils' being turned into snakes and eating the ashy fruit symbolises the great irony that governs the whole poem. Satan and his fellows thought that the single act of disobedience on the part of Adam and Eve would incriminate them utterly and reduce them to their own state of damnation. But Adam and Eve were destined to repent and regain God's favour; and Satan's hopes turned to dust and ashes.

575–7. Milton is here thinking of the many legends of men having to suffer transformation into animals. *man seduced*, 'the seduction of man.'

578–584. This is in itself a strange and far-fetched passage but it serves, by mentioning Eve, as a transition from events in Hell to events in Paradise. Milton followed an old tradition in making the pagan gods the biblical devils in another form; hence the belief that biblical stories might find their way into Greek mythology. The Greek legend here referred to comes in the late Greek epic by Apollonius of Rhodes about the voyage of the Argonauts and the fetching of the Golden Fleece. In this poem, i, 496 ff., Orpheus sang of creation and then "how Ophion and Eurynome, daughter of Ocean, held the sway of snowy Olympus, and how through strength of arm one yielded his prerogative to Saturn and the other to Ops, and how they fell into the waves of Ocean." Ophion means *serpent*, and Eurynome *wide-ruling*; and Milton suggests that the two in conjunction may figure dimly Satan in his serpentine form and Eve, who, in her ambition to reach godhead through eating the fruit, sought to encroach on a power to which she was not entitled.

579. *purchase*, either 'prey,' meaning mankind, or 'gain,' meaning their success in corrupting Adam and Eve. I favour the second interpretation.

583–584. Saturn and Ops were parents of Jove, who was brought up in Crete, where is Mount Dicte.

586. *in power*, 'potentially,' since Adam and Eve were free to sin from the time of their creation.

587. *Once actual*, 'once through an act.' By eating the apple Adam and Eve committed an act of sin, though Sin was not there in person. The last state is for Sin to have her habitual home on earth.

589–590. See *Revelation*, vi, 8, "And behold a pale horse, and his name that sat on him was Death."

593. Understand "is it" before *not*.

599. ravine, 'prey.'

601. *unhide-bound*, 'loose-skinned,' hence 'capacious.'

605. *No homely*, 'choice.'

607. *in man residing through the race*, 'permeating the whole human species,' *through* meaning 'throughout.'

609. In this terrific line we should have in mind both St Paul's "the wages of sin is death" (*Romans*, vi, 23) and the culinary metaphor of *season*. Sin will so thoroughly permeate man that he will become the perfect dish for Death, cooked to a turn and having the final touch of seasoning.

611. *Both* repeats the *both* of the line before and refers to Sin and Death.

617. *havock*, 'destroy without quarter.' *Crying havoc* in a battle was the sign for no quarter.

620. *furies*. The Greek poets had called the Furies of their mythology *dogs*; and it is natural for Milton,

having called Sin and Death dogs, now to call them furies.

624. *conniving* does not include any connotation of covert co-operation and means simply 'letting pass.'

627. *quitted*, 'abandoned.'

630. Milton continues the idea of feeding from the last speech but drops the culinary metaphor in favour of a dog's gluttony as a scavenger of raw offal. Scavengers are useful; and Sin and Death are pictured as useful because they will draw to themselves all the evil incurred through the Fall and enable the Son to commit it all to Hell, thus preparing the way for a purified earth. *draff*, 'dregs' or 'refuse.'

635. Behind this line are the words of *Hosea* (xiii, 14): "I will ransom them from the power of the grave; I will redeem them from death: O death, I will be thy plagues; O grave, I will be thy destruction." This is the passage behind 1 *Corinthians*, xv, 54–56, where Paul again associates sin and death and says that death is swallowed up in victory. Milton has both passages in mind.

638. See Revelation, xxi, 1, "And I saw a new heaven and a new earth."

639. *To*, 'to the extent of.'

640. *both*, 'Heaven and Earth.' *precedes*, 'goes before that happy time.'

645. *extenuate*, 'detract from.' *to the Son, sc.* "they sung."

648. Milton as it were corrects the angels' statement of the new Heaven and Earth rising from the ashes of the old by the statement in *Revelation*, xxi, 2, that the new Jerusalem came down from God out of Heaven.

650. *His mighty angels*, the seven chief archangels, "the seven/Who in God's presence, nearest to his throne/Stand ready at command." (iii, 648–650.)

651. *As sorted best with present things*, 'as best suited the present emergency.'

655. *Decrepit winter*. It was common to personify the seasons, winter being presented as a decrepit old man.

656. *Solstitial summer's heat*, 'the kind of heat to which summer is prone when the days are longest.' *blanc*, 'pale.'

657. *the other five*, the sun and moon being treated as planets according to the Ptolemaic astronomy.

658. *aspects*. Accent on last syllable.

659. "in a sextile (60°), a square (90°), a trine (120°), or opposite (180°) aspect to each other any two planets were regarded as having a harmful influence upon the earth." (M. Y. Hughes.)

661. *In synod unbenign*. When two planets were in conjunction (*synod*), that is, were neighbours in the same sign of the zodiac, their influence was neutral. *fixed*, *sc*. stars.

665. *corners*, 'quarters.' *when*, 'and the times when.'

667. *hall*. Milton here talks of the sky as roofed in (compare the common phrases 'dome' or 'vault of heaven') in order to suggest the impression of the thunder's reverberation.

 668 ff. The main point of these lines is that before the Fall the course of the sun followed the equator of the earth with the result that there were no seasonal variations (in Paradise there was eternal spring). After the Fall the sun's course and the equator were made discrepant, with the result that there were climatic differences. Milton gives two methods by which the change could have happened. Either the earth could have been twisted twenty degrees and more from the sun's axis or the sun's course round the earth could have been twisted the like amount. Milton enlarges on the second method. Masson explains the details of the sun's divergence from its former equatorial circuit as follows: "Milton follows the Sun in imagination . . . first in his ascent north of the equator, through the constellations Taurus (in whose neck are the

Pleiades, called the Seven Atlantic Sisters, as being the daughters of Atlas) and Gemini (called the Spartan twins, as representing Castor and Pollux, sons of Tyndareus, King of Sparta), up to his extreme distance from the equator at the Crab, in the Tropic of Cancer; then returning with him in his descending path by Leo and Virgo, till he again touches the equator with Libra or the Scales; and, for the rest, simply suggesting his similar deviation from the equator to the south by naming the Tropic of Capricorn as the farthest point reached on that side."

671. *the centric globe*, 'the earth, centre of the universe.'

672. Milton uses the classical notion of the sun being driven with a team of horses.

675. *amain*, 'without delay.'

682. *unbenighted*, 'never overtaken by night.'

686. *Estotiland*, a fabulous island near the north-eastern part of North America.

687. *Magellan*, the straits of that name. *At that tasted fruit* 'as soon as the forbidden fruit had been tasted.'

688–689. Atreus hated his brother Thyestes and having got possession of his brother's children invited him to a feast, where the fare was those children's flesh. The sun, unable to bear the sight, was said to have turned his course. *Thyestean*. Accent on second syllable.

690. *though sinless*. Milton implies that this sinlessness was not sufficient to explain the temperate climate of the world before the Fall. There must be a physical explanation such as the one he has just given.

693. *sideral blast*, 'blasting influence of the stars.'

696. *Norumbega*, roughly the area of the state of Maine and its surroundings in North America. *Samoed shore*, a coastal area of the Arctic Ocean stretching from the White Sea into Siberia.

698. *flaw*, 'blast.'

699–700. *Boreas* is the north wind, *Caecias* the north-east, *Argestes* the north-west, and *Thracias* the north-north-west.

702. *Notus* is the south wind, *Afer* the south-west.

703. *Serraliona*, Sierra Leone on the west coast of Africa. *thwart of*, 'across.'

704–706. *Eurus* and *Zephyr* are east and west winds coming from where the sun rises (*Levant*) and sets (*Ponent*) *lateral*. One habitually looks at an atlas or globe with the north uppermost; thus east and west are lateral.

706. *Sirocco*, a hot wind in the Mediterranean area from the south-east. *Libecchio*, 'south-west.'

708. *the irrational*, 'the animals,' which hitherto had been at peace and vegetarians.

719. *disburden* carries on the metaphor of the storm-tost ship. Adam seeks to shed his miseries as a ship jettisons its freight the better to ride the storm.

720. *of*, 'instead of' or 'after being.' Again in 723.

723. Whom does Adam ask to hide him? Probably the shade in which he is already hidden (716). But possibly *O miserable of happy* in 720 is addressed not to himself but to the things of nature generally, and it is these that he asks to hide him. *Surely the first is better.*

726. Note that Adam blames no one but himself; he is not completely Satan's victim.

729. *is propagated curse*, a highly poetical phrase, as easy to grasp as difficult to paraphrase: 'derives from me the incrimination I have incurred.'

738. *Mine own* usually taken to refer back to the curses in 432. But possibly they are his *ill farings* or misfortunes, understood from *Ill fare* in 735. *all from me*, 'all the curses (or misfortunes) that derive from me.'

740–741. When a body has reached its natural place of rest, it should no longer weigh anything, weight consisting of its attraction to that place or centre; and Adam bitterly says that this rule will not apply to him. This amalgamation of a piece of science into a context of high passion is a common characteristic of Donne; and there are other instances in this long speech of Adam. Milton has suffered, first through older critics who censured this passage (and those like it) as unnatural and undignified, and more recently through the more fanatical admirers of Donne, who attacked Milton for not being like Donne even though at times he could be. Actually it is true enough to nature for a mind when wrought up to remember the trivial along with the weighty.

748. *equal*, 'fair.' compare the noun *equity. reduce me to my dust*, 'send me back to the dust from which I was made.'

757. *whatever*, 'whatever they were.'

758. Adam now addresses himself.

759. *cavil*, 'cavil at.'

761. *reproved*, 'if reproved by you.'

764–765. The argument is that a creature deliberately created with a view to his own happiness is more indebted to his creator than is a child, begotten by mere natural necessity and for the begetter's pleasure, to his father. *election*, 'choice.'

771. *whenever*, *sc.* I shall return to dust.

773. *this*. Not strictly correct, for God in *Genesis* said that man would perish on the day of his crime; and a night has now intervened, see line 342.

783. *all*, 'entirely.' Milton may have had in mind Horace's "Non omnis moriar."

785. *inspired*, literally 'breathed in.'

789–792. Adam argues that the body is a mere clod, not to be called alive without the spirit and not responsible, hence not capable of sinning and incurring the punishment of sin. God's sentence applies to the spirit; that sentence is death; therefore the spirit will die.

795. *so*, *i.e.* infinite or endless, hence immortal.

798–801. God is omnipotent; self-contradiction is a sign of weakness; therefore God cannot be self-contradictory.

802. *finite to infinite*, 'mortality to immortality.'

803. *rigour*, 'cruelty.'

805. *dust and nature's law*, 'the law of nature as it apples to dust (the dust to which Adam had been sentenced to return).'

806–808. God's sentence is an agent and it may be assumed that it follows the laws of other agents in the world. These agents vary in their effect according to the capacity of the thing they act on, not according to their own capacity. Imagine two hailstones of equal shape and weight, one falling on concrete, the other on mud. They will have different effects, but these will be due to the different natures of the things that receive them. Similarly if death strikes a geranium and a man, it will be the same death that strikes both; God will not improvise a different kind of death for the special discomfiture of man. Any different effect will be due to the different qualities of the two victims. Milton writes in terms of the scholastic philosophy that still formed a large part of the education at the universities and shows Adam trying by scholastic logic to argue himself out of his fears. Adam's arguments collapse in the next lines when he suspects that he may have been arguing on false premisses concerning the nature of death.

810. *Bereaving sense*, 'abolishing the power of feeling.'

814. *revolution*, 'return.'

816. *am*; "attracted to the nearer and, in Adam's view, more important subject 'I'." (Verity) *incorporate both*, 'lodged together in one body.' Adam now imagines himself forever tied to death, conceived as endless misery.

824. *If guiltless*. Adam in his extremity cannot rest on any

argument; here he at once questions his assumption that his posterity are innocent. *what*, 'what offspring.'

825. *all*, 'totally.' *both mind and will depraved*: either *mind and will* are the subject of *proceed* in the last line; or the whole phrase qualifies Adam's hypothetical posterity and means 'depraved in both mind and will.'

840. *future*. Accent on last syllable.

841. *crime and doom* may be subjects of *are* understood, but, more probably it is Adam who is like Satan both in his sin and his punishment. The irony here is that Adam is wrong and that all unknowing he is not like Satan.

853–854. *since denounced/The day of his offence*: a much compressed and even incorrect phrase, though quite intelligible. It was not (as Milton states) the day that was denounced, i.e. *proclaimed*, but Adam's crime; and the meaning is that death lingers beyond the day when Adam's crime was proclaimed as having incurred the doom of death.

854 ff. Mark the change of tone in this lovely speech. An elegiac note of resignation has replaced the torments of the speech before. Unconsciously Adam begins to relax.

872. *pretended* retains its original Latin meaning of 'held before.' Eve's beauty screens her *hellish falsehood*.

875. *wandering*, 'unstable.'

878–879. him overweening/To overreach, 'being overconfident in your power to overreach him.'

886. *sinister* bears both its literal and metaphorical sense. Eve was fashioned from a rib taken from Adam's *left* side, and she was an *unlucky* creation.

887–888. Adam was thought to have had thirteen ribs on his left side and in the interests of uniformity to have benefited by losing one for the fashioning of Eve. *iust* could mean either 'even' or 'correct' or both.

896. More mischiefs that will befall mankind could have been avoided.

898. *strait*, 'close.'

905. *already linked* probably refers to the unlucky man who finds his true mate too late after he has been united to an incompatible wife, whom he hates. But it could also refer to the true mate.

910. As Eve was first responsible for the Fall, so Milton makes her take the initiative in extricating herself and Adam from its dire consequences.

924–925. *Joining . . . one enmity*, a telescoped phrase, 'joining our separate enmities into one enmity.'

938. I do not agree with M. Y. Hughes that *Immovable* qualifies Adam, 'who is inflexible until Eve's confession of her fault brings *peace* between them,' and find it more natural that it should qualify *plight*. Eve's *lowly plight* is her posture of humility, and this she refuses to change until she has got Adam's pardon.

938–939. *from fault/Acknowledged and deplored*, 'through admitting and deploring her fault.'

953. *place*, see 932.

955. Adam goes back completely on his earlier, bitter, speech to Eve.

961. *in our share of woe*, 'through the way in which each shares the other's burden.'

962. *this day's death denounced*, 'the death that has been declared for us this day.'

965. *derived*, 'transmitted.'

967. *experiment*, 'experience.'

969. *event*, 'consequence.'

976–977. *extremes*, 'extremity.' *relief* and *end* are explained in the lines that follow. It will be a relief of their extremity if by avoiding offspring they confine God's punishment to themselves, and it will be an end of it if they commit suicide.

978. *As in our evils*, 'considering the evil plight we are in.' A Latinism, *ut in*.

979. *descent*, 'descendants.'

987. *prevent*, 'cut off in advance.'

996. Eve herself, who stands before him.

1000. *make short*, 'make short work of it.'

1004. *and have the power*, 'while we have the power.'

1006. 'to destroy the destructive power of death by destroying ourselves.'

1013–1028. Adam means that Eve's spurning of life and pleasure has something truly heroic in it, but not when it leads to sterility or suicide. Milton is thinking of the sufferings of martyrs and fighters in a good cause as the true heroism, which Eve's protests may foreshadow. *Self-destruction* (line 1016) must mean here not suicide but destruction of part of their own potentialities, namely of their power to have children; and this is an act not of deliberate valour but of unbalanced despair. Suicide (*if thou covet death*), too, is not truly heroic but a vain attempt to circumvent God's purposes.

1045. *reluctance*, 'struggling.'

1052–1053. *with joy,/Fruit of thy womb*, a compressed phrase. Understand *with* before *fruit*. Eve will be recompensed with joy and with the child she bears, in other words with joy over the child when born. This seems better than to understand *fruit* as in apposition to *joy*.

1053–1054. See lines 201–208. Adam says that the curse there pronounced did not hit him directly but fell obliquely, grazed him merely, and fell mainly on the earth.

1065. *this mountain*. Paradise was set on a hill.

1068. *shroud*, 'protection.'

1069. *diurnal star*, 'the sun.'

1070. Before *how* understand *seek* from 1067.

1070–1071. *gathered beams reflected*. *reflected* in Milton's day could mean *bent* as well as *mirrored*, and the strange idea of the sun's rays being first focussed by means of a lens and then mirrored onto tinder is not necessary. The phrase probably means 'beams that have been bent from their direct path to make a cluster.' *sere*, 'dry.' *foment*, 'foster into heat.'

1073. *attrite*, 'by friction.'

1075. *tine*, 'kindle.' *thwart*, 'oblique.'

1077. *comfortable*, 'comforting.'

1078. *supply*, 'supplement.'

1081–1082. *praying . . . beseeching*, 'if we pray . . . if we beseech.'

1082–1083. *need not fear/To pass*, 'need have no fears about passing.'

1091. *frequenting*, 'crowding.' *contrite*. Accent on last syllable.